YOUR MIND: TRANSLATED

YOUR MIND TRANSLATED

YOUR MIND EDITS REALITY—AND YOU CALL IT TRUTH.

JACK HERNANDEZ

Copyright © 2025 by Jack Hernandez

All rights reserved. No part of this publication may be reproduced or distributed in any form or by any means, or stored in a database or retrieval system, without prior written consent. Requests for material to reproduce material from this work should be sent to: yourmindtranslatedbook@gmail.com .

DEDICATION

To M.S

Your love has been the quiet foundation beneath every word in this book. Through my late nights of writing, moments of creative struggle, and the vulnerable process of translating thoughts into meaning, you remained my anchor and my inspiration. Your faith in me and in this work gave me the courage to believe that these ideas are worth sharing. This book carries your heart within its pages.

This work is also dedicated to every reader who has chosen to spend their precious time with these words—whether you purchased this book, borrowed it from a friend, discovered it in a library, or read just a few pages in passing. Time is our most valuable gift, and the fact that you've shared even a moment of yours with my humble attempt to explore the human mind moves me beyond words. Though I may claim no great originality, I am deeply honored that you've allowed these thoughts to occupy space in your day, your mind, and perhaps your heart. Your attention and engagement give this work its true meaning and purpose.

Thank you.

Table of Contents

FOREWORD 1
CHAPTER ONE : Identifying Yourself with Thoughts 3
CHAPTER TWO : Our Lying Eyes 20
CHAPTER THREE : Our Deaf Ears 47
CHAPTER FOUR : Our Senses/The Senses 70
CHAPTER FIVE : Language 108
CHAPTER SIX : Connection Mind/Body 146
CHAPTER SEVEN : Relationships 185
CHAPTER EIGHT : The Absolute Truth 227
A NOTE FROM THE AUTHOR 263
ACKNOWLEDGMENTS 265

FOREWORD

YOUR MIND: TRANSLATED

As you're reading these words, your mind is working to figure out what this short book is all about. Your brain—that is, your "mind"—is doing what it does best: analyzing, connecting dots, and making sense of these words.

Despite its reputation as an incredibly sophisticated piece of organic machinery, your brain is a terrible interpreter of reality. While your eyes are busily scanning these lines and your brain is processing all this information, millions of microprocesses are happening in the background, making assumptions and judgments—but not getting all of them right. In fact, most of them are just making wild guesses and hoping for the best.

Let's take a moment. Really—just sit with it. Funny thing is, even as I say that your brain's already off and running, doing its thing without asking you first. It's not waiting for permission. It's more like a hyperactive roommate narrating everything, whether you're paying attention or not. You think you're steering the wheel, but most of the time, you're just along for the ride.

FOREWORD

Right now, you might be asking yourself, "Have I spent my whole life letting my brain translate my experiences without ever questioning whether it's doing a good job?" That's exactly the questions that this book explores. We're going to dig deep into this squishy, gray mass we call a brain, break down its role as our personal (and often faulty) translator, and figure out why we trust it so blindly.

By understanding how your mind works—and how it misleads you—you'll gain practical insights that can transform how you:

- Respond to difficult emotions
- Interact with others
- Make decisions
- Find genuine happiness

So, if you're ready to question everything you thought you knew about yourself, your mind, and the world around you, then let's dive in.

CHAPTER ONE

IDENTIFYING YOURSELF WITH THOUGHTS

"The primary cause of unhappiness is never the situation but your thoughts about it."
— Eckhart Tolle[1]

Have you ever noticed how busy your mind is? Right now, as you read these words, a constant commentary is happening in the background of your awareness. For example, you might be thinking "I like this idea," "This reminds me of something I read before," "I wonder if this will really help me," or "I should check my phone." These thoughts arise spontaneously, one after another, like waves on an ocean.

Many philosophers and spiritual teachers throughout history—from the Buddha to Epictetus to Eckhart Tolle— have suggested that we often rely too heavily on our "minds" for everything. From making decisions to designing buildings and even launching rockets, we place enormous trust in the interpreter inside our heads. Because of this constant reliance, we've developed a dangerous habit: We confuse our minds with who we are.

THE MIND AS A TOOL, NOT YOUR IDENTITY

Think of your mind as a sophisticated tool that is similar to a high-tech translation device. It helps you interpret your environment, process information, and communicate with others. But just like any tool, it can malfunction, need maintenance, or simply not be suited for every job.

When our mind feels upset, happy, or sad, we often believe that we experiencing these emotions. But there's a crucial distinction here: Your mind is generating these feelings in response to its interpretation of events—interpretations that may be flawed or incomplete.

The Interpreter Within

Neuroscientist Michael Gazzaniga's research on split-brain patients revealed what he called "the interpreter" in the left hemisphere—a mechanism that constantly creates explanations for our behaviors, even when it doesn't have access to the real reasons.[2] (A split-brain patient is one whose corpus callosum has severed, thus disconnecting the two halves of the brain.) In one famous experiment, a split-brain patient was shown two images simultaneously—a snow scene to the right visual field (processed by the left hemisphere) and a chicken claw to the left visual field (processed by the right hemisphere). When asked to point to images related to what they saw, the patient's left hand pointed to a shovel (related to snow) while the right hand pointed to a chicken. When asked to explain this choice, the patient said, "Oh, that's simple. The chicken claw goes with the chicken, and you need a shovel to clean out the chicken shed."

The left hemisphere had no access to the snow scene but created a logical explanation anyway. This interpreter function operates in all of us, constantly crafting stories to explain our experiences.

Consider a time when someone said something that upset you. Maybe it was an offhand comment that bothered you for days, or something you overheard that made you uncomfortable. It's easy to believe the other person caused your feelings. In reality, though, you control your reactions. The power to decide how to respond resides in your mind.

Picture this scenario: You're waiting for a friend at a café. They're 20 minutes late, and you haven't received any message explaining why. Your mind might start generating thoughts: "They don't respect my time." "They don't value

IDENTIFYING YOURSELF WITH THOUGHTS

our friendship." "Something terrible has happened to them." Each of these thoughts creates a different emotional reaction—anger, hurt, or worry. But none of these interpretations may be true. Perhaps their phone died, they got caught in unexpected traffic, or they wrote down the wrong time.

This simple example illustrates how your mind creates interpretations that feel absolutely real to you. The emotions these thoughts generate—the anger, hurt, or worry—feel just as real. Yet they're all based on a story your mind has constructed without complete information.

When you truly understand how your thoughts and feelings work, you experience a profound sense of freedom. True freedom comes when you recognize that no one can upset you because you know yourself and how your mind operates.

The Mirror Effect: Projecting Our Inner World

"Everything that irritates us about others can lead us to an understanding of ourselves."
— **Carl Jung** [3]

Thinking can trap us in the belief that we are separate from others. This belief leads to constant comparisons and self-imposed limitations. The more we identify with our thoughts, the further we drift from thinking critically and understanding our true selves.

Michael Jackson once encouraged us to "start with the man in the mirror" if we want to change the world. But what if that mirror is cloudy? What if the reflection you see isn't really you, but rather what society expects? This experience can be unsettling, especially if that distorted image influences your choices.

We often mirror each other. We project our own unresolved problems—our fears and insecurities—onto others, blaming them for things that actually reflect our inner struggles. This psychological phenomenon, known as *projection*, was extensively studied by the Swiss psychiatrist Carl Jung, who noted that the qualities we most strongly react to in others are often the ones we deny or repress in ourselves.[3]

The Shadow Self

Jung coined the term "shadow self" to refer to the aspects of our personality that we've pushed into our unconscious because they conflict with how we want to see ourselves. For example, a person who prides themselves on being honest may be particularly triggered by perceived dishonesty in others. Someone who suppresses their anger may find themselves surrounded by "angry people."

IDENTIFYING YOURSELF WITH THOUGHTS

Consider Sarah, a meticulous planner who takes pride in her organizational skills. When her more spontaneous colleague Ryan suggests impromptu changes to a project, Sarah feels intensely irritated. "He's so irresponsible and chaotic," she thinks. Sarah doesn't recognize that part of her irritation stems from her own repressed desire for spontaneity and freedom from rigid structures—qualities she has denied in herself but unconsciously admires in Ryan.

By becoming aware of these projections, we gain valuable insights into our own psychological makeup. When you find yourself having an intense emotional reaction to someone else's behavior, ask yourself: "Is there any part of me that is like this too?" The answer can be illuminating and often humbling.

When you choose not to be hurt by what others say or do, you free yourself from needless pain. Each day, it's important to work on directing your mind, finding constructive ways to think, and accepting reality. Fighting against what is real only causes unnecessary suffering.

THE PARADOX OF LIMITED PERCEPTION

"We don't see things as they are; we see them as we are."
— Anaïs Nin[4]

Although the world seems full of endless possibilities, our perspective is remarkably limited. We can see only three dimensions and a small range of colors, and we process information through only five senses. For a long time, we thought that our perceptions represented all of reality. But our perceptions are really just tiny windows that can trap our imaginations.

The Constraints of Human Perception

Consider the mantis shrimp, which has sixteen color receptors compared to our mere three. It perceives colors we cannot even imagine.[5] Dolphins use echolocation (reflected sound) to "see" through objects. Bats navigate in complete darkness using sound waves. These creatures experience aspects of reality that are completely inaccessible to us.

Even within our limited range of perception, we don't consciously register most of what our senses detect. Our retinas receive approximately 10 million bits of information every second, yet our conscious minds process only about 40 bits.[6] Our brains filter out the rest as "irrelevant." This means that 99.9996% of the available sensory information never reaches our conscious awareness.

Think about that for a moment. Your reality—what you believe is "out there"—is constructed from less than 0.0004% of the available information. That tiny fraction is processed, interpreted, and distorted by your mind based on your past experiences, beliefs, and expectations.

Even though we believe we see reality clearly, what we observe is just a small fraction of what exists. This raises an important question: Can we truly trust our senses—what we see, hear, smell, touch, and feel? Often, our choices are influenced by impulses and biases that operate below our conscious awareness.

The Multiple Voices of Mind

Although we might believe there is one guiding voice in our minds, countless processes are happening simultaneously, most of which we never notice. Neuroscientist David Eagleman compares the brain to a team of rivals, with different neural systems competing for control of our behavior.[7] The brain is extremely complex, working tirelessly behind the scenes, but we remain unaware of much of what it does.

In a famous study by Benjamin Libet, participants were asked to flex their wrists whenever they felt the urge to do so. Electrodes measured both their brain activity and muscle movement. Astonishingly, the brain activity indicating a decision occurred 350 milliseconds *before* the participants reported feeling the urge to move.[8] This finding suggests that what we experience as conscious decision-making may actually be our awareness catching up to decisions already made by unconscious processes in our brains.

We are like Pinocchio, believing we're in control, while unseen forces pull the strings.

The Evolutionary Mismatch

The human brain isn't built for success; it's built for survival. Survival means conserving energy, while success often requires expending energy and facing discomfort. Our brains evolved in an environment vastly different from today's world—one where calorie conservation was crucial, immediate threats were common, and social acceptance meant the difference between life and death.

Psychologist Robert Kurzban explains that the mind is not a unified entity but rather a collection of specialized mechanisms that evolved to solve specific adaptive problems.[9] These mechanisms often operate according to different priorities and can come into conflict with one another. For example, your desire to lose weight conflicts with your craving for sugar. Your commitment to finish a project clashes with your urge to check social media. These conflicts aren't failures of willpower; they're the natural consequence of a brain designed for a different world.

Struggling with procrastination or making self-defeating choices doesn't mean you're broken or defective. It means your brain is working exactly as it was designed to. Success requires changing how your brain operates.

We become what we think about most. This is why it's so important to think rationally and have clear goals. Throughout history, people have sought to connect with something greater than themselves—what philosophers, including Jung, called the "collective unconscious."[3] However, we often get so distracted by our thoughts that we forget what really matters.

The Paradox of Scale

With over 8 billion people in the world, our individual lives may seem small, but our choices and actions can profoundly affect others. For instance, depending on your current mindset, this book might transform how you see your life and help you overcome challenges—or it might not resonate with you at all.

This paradox of scale—that we are simultaneously infinitesimal in the cosmic perspective yet immensely significant in our immediate sphere of influence—can be difficult to reconcile. This tension is beautifully captured by astronauts who have experienced the "overview effect"—a cognitive shift reported by those who have viewed Earth from space. Edgar Mitchell, the sixth person to walk on the moon, described it the overview effect as "an instant global consciousness, a people orientation, an intense dissatisfaction with the state of the world, and a compulsion to do something about it."[10]

Many conflicts arise when people feel like victims or refuse to take charge of their thoughts. Instead of taking responsibility for their mental patterns, they blame others. However, Viktor Frankl, who survived Nazi concentration camps, observed that even in the most horrific circumstances, individuals retain "the last of human freedoms—to choose one's attitude in any given set of circumstances."[11]

Life is complicated—sometimes it makes sense, and sometimes it doesn't. We often think we're the center of the universe, but in reality, we're tiny pieces in a vast, complex reality. In many ways, we still have the curiosity of children, but we are weighed down by adult responsibilities and forget the joy of dreaming.

THE SHIP OF THESEUS: IDENTITY OVER TIME

We do not remain the same people over time. Every seven to ten years, most of our organs and cells regenerate completely, so the body you had a decade ago no longer exists.[12] We are like a brick wall that is rebuilt daily—after

IDENTIFYING YOURSELF WITH THOUGHTS

ten years, it may still stand, but is it the same wall? Even though we physically change, we cling to who we think we were.

This philosophical paradox, known as the Ship of Theseus, poses an important question: If you replace every plank of a ship one by one until no original parts remain, is it still the same ship? Similarly, if your body's cells have been entirely replaced, and many of your beliefs, preferences, and memories have changed, are you the same person you were as a child?[13]

Despite the physical and psychological transformations that humans undergo, most of us maintain a strong sense of continuous identity. We believe we are the same "self" moving through time. This continuity is largely a narrative construction—a story we tell ourselves about who we are. Although this story provides useful coherence in our lives, identifying too strongly with it can limit our potential for growth and change.

In today's world, we often feel trapped by the identities we create for ourselves. We feel judged by how much we can do or own. However, true happiness doesn't come from what you accomplish but instead from how well you do things. The process is more important than the end result.

The Minefield of the Mind

Humans often fall into their own mental traps, influenced by biases and blind spots. Indeed, our thinking is riddled with biases—those subtle, ingrained prejudices that distort our perception of the world. We also have blind spots, areas where we lack awareness, where we fail to see the full picture. "An uncontrolled mind is like a dangerous minefield—it can blow us to smithereens."

Psychologist Daniel Kahneman's research has revealed that our minds operate in two distinct modes: System 1 (fast, intuitive, emotional) and System 2 (slow, deliberate, logical).[14] Most of our daily decisions are handled by System 1, which relies on mental shortcuts (called *heuristics*) that work well enough most of the time but can lead to systematic errors in judgment.

Consider these common cognitive biases:

- **Confirmation bias**: We seek and favor information that confirms our existing beliefs while ignoring contradictory evidence.
- **Availability heuristic**: We overestimate the likelihood of events we can easily recall, usually because they're recent or emotionally charged.
- **Negativity bias**: We give more weight to negative experiences than to positive experiences.

IDENTIFYING YOURSELF WITH THOUGHTS

- **Dunning-Kruger effect**: People with low ability in a specific area tend to overestimate their ability, while experts tend to underestimate their abilities relative to others.[15]

These biases aren't character flaws; they're features of our cognitive architecture. Recognizing them doesn't eliminate them, but awareness creates the possibility of counteracting their influence on our decisions.

Understanding our cognitive architecture is important because this architecture isn't fixed—our brains are constantly being shaped by the world around us. Think of it this way: Your brain is a garden, and your experiences are the gardeners. Every interaction, every piece of information, every sight and sound acts as a gardener, pruning some neural pathways, nurturing others, and ultimately shaping the landscape of your mind.

The people around us are particularly influential gardeners. They plant seeds of expectation, cultivate norms of behavior, and prune away thoughts and actions that don't conform. Because we are social creatures to our core, wired to connect and belong, we are extremely susceptible to the influence of others, both consciously and unconsciously. We mirror their behaviors, adopt their beliefs, and internalize their values. Social influence can be a powerful force for good, fostering cooperation and community. But it can also lead us astray, trapping us in echo chambers of conformity and limiting our potential for independent thought.

In essence, we are walking contradictions—individuals shaped by social environments, with minds constantly molded by external forces. Navigating this complex interplay requires a delicate balance: embracing the positive aspects of social influence while cultivating the self-awareness to recognize and challenge our biases, to defuse the minefields within our own minds. We are on a lifelong journey of self-discovery, of learning to navigate the intricate landscape of our inner and outer worlds.

PRACTICE: REFRAMING YOUR THOUGHTS

Take five minutes today to notice and reframe your negative thoughts. When you notice yourself thinking "I am angry" or "I am anxious," try thinking instead "I notice anger arising" or "I'm experiencing anxiety right now." This small shift in perspective can create space between you and your thoughts, allowing you to respond more intentionally rather than react automatically.

This practice, derived from mindfulness meditation traditions, is supported by contemporary research showing that this kind of *cognitive defusion*—creating psychological distance between yourself and your thoughts—can reduce

IDENTIFYING YOURSELF WITH THOUGHTS

emotional reactivity and improve psychological well-being.[16] By reframing your thoughts as passing mental events rather than absolute truths about reality, you begin to loosen their grip on your emotions and behavior.

> "Between stimulus and response, there is a space. In that space is our power to choose our response. In our response lies our growth and our freedom."
> — **Viktor Frankl** [11]

As we conclude this chapter, consider how fundamentally your thoughts shape your experience of reality. Your mind is constantly translating raw sensory data into a coherent narrative that you call "my life." But this translation is influenced by your past experiences, cultural conditioning, evolutionary biases, and countless other factors beyond your conscious awareness.

By becoming aware of this translation process, you gain the freedom to question and revise it. You begin to see that your thoughts are not absolute truths but rather interpretations of reality—interpretations that can be changed. This awareness is the first step toward a more conscious and intentional relationship with your own mind.

In the next chapter, we explore how this translation process affects our most fundamental sense—vision. As you'll discover, what you see with your own eyes may not be what you think it is.

CHAPTER TWO

OUR LYING EYES

"The eye sees only what the mind is prepared to comprehend."
— Robertson Davies[1]

Have you ever noticed images circulating on the internet that seem to be one thing but can transform into something entirely different depending on how you look at them? For example, consider the classic image known as the Duck-Rabbit illusion:

When you look at this image, you might see either a duck or a rabbit. What's fascinating is that while you can consciously switch between seeing one or the other, it's nearly impossible to see both simultaneously. The crucial point to remember is this: While the sensory information remains the same, your perception can vary drastically. Your brain constructs and translates your perceptions continuously. This means that while sensations are real, our perceptions may not be. In other words, how you see the world, people, and situations might not accurately reflect their true nature.

THE DUCK AND THE RABBIT: PERCEPTION VERSUS REALITY

The Duck-Rabbit illusion was popularized by philosopher Ludwig Wittgenstein to demonstrate how a single object can be interpreted in multiple ways.[2] This simple drawing reveals something profound about human perception: We don't passively receive visual information. Instead, we actively construct what we see based on context, expectations, and past experiences.

Think about what's happening in your brain when you look at the Duck-Rabbit image. The actual visual input—the lines on the page—doesn't change. But your interpretation of those lines shifts dramatically depending on whether you're seeing the duck or the rabbit. This interpretive process happens so quickly and automatically that you're rarely aware of it.

The philosopher Maurice Merleau-Ponty described perception not as a passive reception of information but as an active engagement with the world.[3] We don't simply see; we look. We don't merely hear; we listen. Our perceptions are shaped by our intentions, expectations, and the meaning we assign to what we encounter.

This active construction of perception applies not just to ambiguous images like the Duck-Rabbit but to everything we experience. The face of a loved one, a beautiful sunset, a political speech, a work of art—all are constructed by our minds based on much more than the raw sensory data entering our eyes and ears.

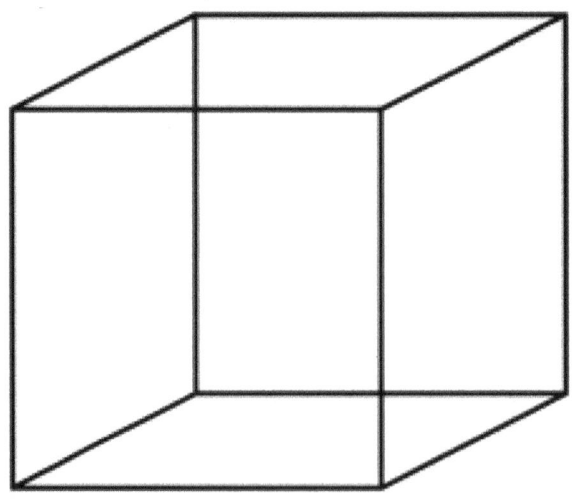

The Necker Cube: Another Window into Perception

Consider another classic ambiguous image, the Necker Cube:

This simple wireframe drawing of a cube can be perceived in two different ways: with the front face appearing at either the bottom left or the top right. As with the Duck-Rabbit, you can consciously switch between these two interpretations, but it's difficult to maintain both simultaneously.

What's happening here? The lines themselves don't change, but your perception of their three-dimensional arrangement does. Your brain automatically fills in missing information—in this case, depth cues—to create a coherent three-dimensional perception from two-dimensional input.[4]

Even more striking is what happens when you stare at the Necker Cube for an extended period. Eventually, your perception will begin to switch involuntarily between the two possible interpretations. This phenomenon, known as *bistable perception*, reveals that even when you're trying to maintain a single interpretation, your brain continues to explore alternative ways of organizing the same visual information.[5]

THE BIOLOGY OF VISION: A COMPLEX PROCESS

Let's take a moment to appreciate the astonishing complexity of vision—a process we often take for granted. Far from being a simple camera-like recording of the world, vision involves multiple stages of processing, filtering, and interpretation.

The eye is the primary sensory organ responsible for vision. Light waves travel across the cornea and enter the eye through the pupil. The cornea, a transparent covering over the eye, acts as a barrier between the inner eye and the outside world while also focusing light waves. The pupil, a small opening in the eye, can change size based on light levels and emotional arousal. In low light, the pupil dilates, or expands, to allow more light to enter. Conversely, in bright light, the pupil constricts to limit the amount of light entering the eye. The pupil's size is controlled by muscles connected to the iris, which is the colored part of the eye. That's just one eye with many moving parts! Once light enters, visual information passes through the lens, which focuses it onto the retina at the back of the eye. The retina contains approximately 126 million photoreceptors—specialized cells called rods and cones (rods take care of black/white while cones are for colors) that convert light into electrical signals.[6] These signals are then transmitted through the optic nerve to the brain.

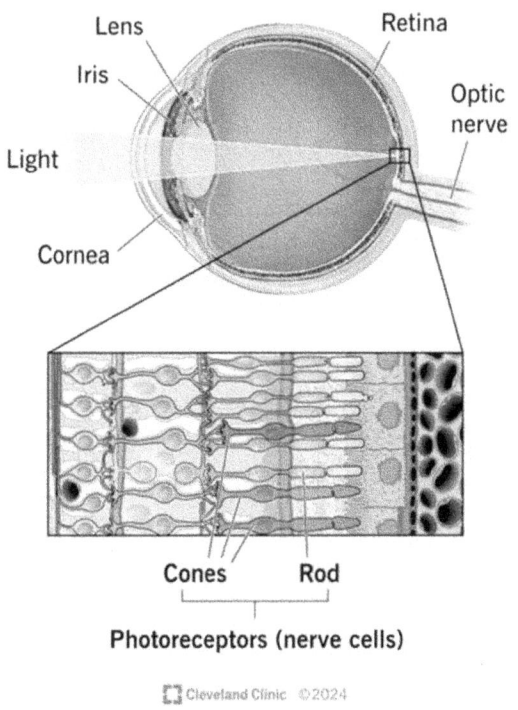

The human eye.

But the journey has only just begun. The signals travel to the thalamus, a relay station in the brain, and then on to the primary visual cortex in the occipital lobe. From there, visual information is processed along two main pathways: the *what pathway* (ventral stream), which is involved in object recognition and identification, and the *where/how pathway* (dorsal stream), which deals with spatial awareness and interaction with visual stimuli.[7]

At each stage of this process, the brain is not simply relaying information but rather actively transforming it—enhancing certain features, suppressing others, comparing current input with stored memories, and integrating information from other senses and cognitive processes.

This process is extremely complex, but that's exactly the point. It takes an enormous amount of energy and a multitude of processes to handle even a single beam of light entering our brains. Yet, our minds like to believe that no "errors" occur in this process.

The Blind Spot: A Revealing Flaw

To appreciate how actively your brain constructs your visual experience, consider the blind spot—a natural gap in your vision caused by the optic nerve. Where the optic nerve connects to the retina, there are no photoreceptors, creating a small blind spot in each eye.[8]

Try this simple experiment:

+   ●

1. Close your right eye and focus your left eye on the cross.
2. Hold the book about 20 inches from your face.
3. Slowly move the book closer while keeping your eye on the cross.
4. At a certain distance, the dot will disappear as it falls on your blind spot.

   What's remarkable isn't that you have a blind spot—it's that you never notice it in daily life. Your brain seamlessly fills in this gap with information from the surrounding visual field, creating the illusion of a complete and continuous visual world. This filling-in happens automatically and unconsciously, demonstrating how your brain constructs rather than merely records your visual experience.

BEHAVIORAL INFLUENCES ON PERCEPTION

Our perceptions are shaped not only by the physical structure of our sensory organs but also by behavioral and social factors. The way we see the world is profoundly influenced by our evolutionary history, cultural context, and even the behaviors of those around us.

For instance, the blue stripe on the edge of the belly of the male fence lizard can provoke aggressive behavior in other males. Females lack this marking and are not attacked. However, if you paint a blue pattern on a female, she will be immediately attacked. Conversely, if you remove the stripe from a male, he will be courted instead of attacked.[9]

This example from the animal kingdom demonstrates how visual cues can bypass conscious evaluation and trigger automatic behavioral responses. The male lizards don't "decide" to attack after careful consideration—they react automatically to the blue stripe, which serves as a stimulus that triggers an innate response.

Humans, though more complex, aren't so different in this regard and also tend to mirror the behaviors of those around them. If we see others moving in a particular direction, we may be tempted to move in that direction too. If someone yawns, we might feel tired too. Even witnessing looters can turn people who normally oppose such actions into looters themselves.

The Power of Social Influence on Perception

The famous conformity experiments conducted by Solomon Asch demonstrated how social pressure can literally change what people perceive—or at least what they're willing to report perceiving.[10] In these studies, participants were asked to match the length of a line with one of three comparison lines. When alone, participants rarely made errors. But when placed in a group where confederates deliberately gave wrong answers, many participants conformed to the group's incorrect judgment, despite the evidence of their own eyes.

More recent research using functional MRI has shown that social influence can actually alter activity in the visual cortex, suggesting that social pressure doesn't just change our reported perceptions but may actually modify how our brains process visual information.[11]

This influence extends beyond laboratory settings. Think about fashion trends, for example. What looks attractive or stylish often depends less on objective visual qualities and more on social consensus. A clothing style that seems bizarre or unappealing can become desirable once it's adopted by enough influential people.

The Baby Face: Hardwired Visual Preferences

Konrad Lorenz's "baby face" theory provides another fascinating example of how visual cues influence our perceptions. Features such as a relatively large head, large eyes positioned low, chubby cheeks, and plump extremities make animals and dolls appear more lovable and cuter. These characteristics, which Lorenz called *kindchenschema* (baby schema), trigger nurturing responses across cultures.[12]

Toys and cartoon characters, like those from Disney, often exaggerate these traits, creating appealing figures to which most people respond positively. Just imagine if Mickey Mouse had an adult mouse head or sharp claws—he wouldn't seem so cute anymore, would he?

This isn't just a quirk of human preference; it's a deeply ingrained perceptual bias with evolutionary roots. Humans who felt protective toward infants with these features were more likely to ensure their survival, passing down genes that predisposed future generations to respond positively to the same visual cues.

OBSERVATION AS CREATION

"The world of the happy is quite different from that of the unhappy."
— **Ludwig Wittgenstein**[13]

Observation is an act of creation limited by the inherent constraints of our thinking. By labeling and naming, we create illusions about the world. Naming something restricts it, limiting its potential. We rarely see anything in its entirety because reality consists of layers upon layers of efficiently constructed visual stimuli. Consequently, what we perceive is often a diluted version of what life truly is.

To observe is to create, but it's a creation born of limitations. Our thinking, powerful as it is, comes with inherent constraints. We categorize, we label, we name—and in doing so, we construct illusions about the world. When we give something a name, we define it, but we also confine it. We reduce its vast potential to a single, limited concept.

The Naming of Things

Imagine a child encountering the ocean for the first time. Before learning the word "ocean," they experience it as a boundless expanse of blue, a mysterious and awe-inspiring entity. But once they learn to call it "ocean," it becomes a defined body of water, categorized and filed away in their mind. The boundless wonder, the sense of limitless possibility, is subtly diminished.

The power of naming to shape perception is evident in an experiment conducted by psychologist Paul Rozin. He presented participants with two identical bottles of sugar, labeling one as "sugar" and the other as "sodium cyanide (poison)." Despite knowing intellectually that both bottles contained harmless sugar, many participants refused to drink from the bottle labeled "poison."[14] The label itself changed their perception of the substance, overriding their factual knowledge.

This process of labeling and categorizing is essential for navigating the world. It allows us to communicate, to make sense of our surroundings, and to build mental models of reality. But it also creates a veil between us and the true nature of things. We rarely, if ever, perceive anything in its entirety.

The Map Is Not the Territory

The Polish American scientist Alfred Korzybski famously stated, "The map is not the territory."[15] By this, he meant that our mental representations of reality (our "maps") are not the same as reality itself (the "territory"). Our perceptions and concepts are abstractions, simplified models that can never capture the full complexity of what they represent.

Think of reality as an intricate tapestry, woven with countless threads of visual stimuli. Like a magnifying glass, our senses focus on a small section of this tapestry, highlighting certain threads while obscuring others. Our minds then weave these highlighted threads into a coherent narrative, a simplified representation of the whole. This is the "diluted" version of reality we perceive—a necessary simplification, perhaps, but a simplification nonetheless.

You are the lens through which creation observes itself—a conscious aperture filtering the infinite into something knowable, shaping the vast complexity of existence into a story you can live, feel, and understand. Through you, the universe becomes aware of its own beauty and chaos, its patterns and mysteries. You don't see reality as it is; you see it as it passes through the unique filter of your mind, your history, and your emotions. In this way, perception is both a mirror and a masterpiece—reflecting what is, while simultaneously creating what seems to be.

The Observer Effect

In quantum physics, the observer effect refers to the concept that the mere act of observation can change what's being observed.[16] While often misunderstood or oversimplified in popular culture, this principle points to a profound truth about perception: The act of looking is not passive but interactive.

Consider how your attention changes your experience. If you focus on the negative aspects of a situation, they become more prominent in your perception. If you look for beauty in your surroundings, you'll find more of it. Your attention doesn't just select from what's there; it actively shapes what you experience.

This is not to suggest that reality is entirely subjective or that we can simply think our way into a different world. The tapestry exists independent of our perception. But the part of it we see—and how we interpret what we see—is profoundly shaped by where and how we look.

BEAUTY IN THE EYE OF THE BEHOLDER

Much of what we perceive exists solely in our minds, which can make it difficult to express our perceptions to others.

The question, "Why do we find this beautiful and not that?" transforms into a more profound inquiry: "Why do humans perceive this particular thing as beautiful and that as ugly?" The explanation for our aesthetic experiences lies not in the form of the stimuli but in the structure of the nervous systems that receive them. Therefore, beauty may not exist independently of human perception.

Cultural Variations in Beauty

Cross-cultural studies reveal fascinating differences in aesthetic preferences. For example, the Maasai people of East Africa traditionally considered elongated earlobes beautiful, while in parts of Myanmar, the Kayan people valued elongated necks created by wearing brass coils. [17] In Renaissance Europe, pale skin and fuller figures were considered beautiful, while contemporary Western culture often prizes tanned skin and slender physiques.

These dramatic variations suggest that beauty is not an inherent quality of objects or people but rather a product of cultural conditioning and collective agreement. What we find attractive is largely learned through socialization and exposure to cultural standards.

Yet some aspects of beauty perception appear to transcend cultural boundaries. Studies suggest that facial symmetry, clear skin, and certain body proportions are consistently associated with attractiveness across cultures, possibly reflecting evolutionary adaptations related to health and fertility.[18] We therefore see a complex interplay between biological predispositions and cultural learning in shaping our aesthetic judgments.

The Self-Fulfilling Prophecy of Beauty

Our perceptions of beauty can create self-fulfilling prophecies. Research has demonstrated what psychologists call the *beauty premium* or *attractiveness bias* — the tendency to attribute positive qualities to attractive people and treat them more favorably.[19] People perceived as attractive are often assumed to be more intelligent, competent, and likable, even without evidence to support these assumptions.

These assumptions then affect how we interact with others, which in turn influences their behavior. If we expect someone to be competent and likable because they're attractive, we may treat them in ways that encourage confidence and social ease, thereby reinforcing our initial perception.

Consider how this cycle might work: A child perceived as attractive receives more positive attention and encouragement, developing greater social confidence. This confidence makes them more appealing to others, reinforcing both their own self-image and others' perception of them as attractive and likable. The initial perception has helped create the reality it claimed to merely observe.

Seeing Through the Illusion

We do not see the world directly; instead, we interpret it through the filters of our senses and minds. In doing so, we categorize people and things, assigning labels that help us make sense of our environment. But this tendency to label doesn't stop at the external world—it extends inward, shaping how we see ourselves. As a result, many of us try to define and enhance our identity through material possessions, using them as symbols of worth, status, and belonging. We begin to seek validation not from within, but from what the world reflects back at us.

The philosopher Alain de Botton suggests that much of our suffering stems from comparing ourselves to others and feeling inadequate as a result. Yet the lens through which we view others is rarely neutral. The influencer whose life appears flawless, the colleague who seems effortlessly successful, the couple who radiate happiness—these images are shaped not only by careful curation, but also by our own insecurities, projections, and longing.

Psychologists also note that comparison isn't always self-defeating. Through a phenomenon known as *downward comparison*, we may seek comfort by focusing on those we perceive as worse off. A student who earns a B- might feel consoled by the fact that friends received C's. But whether comparison lifts us up or pulls us down, the result is the same: We measure our worth not by who we are, but by where we stand in relation to others. In doing so, we risk losing sight of ourselves in a mirror that was never ours to begin with.

By recognizing the constructed nature of our perceptions, we can begin to loosen their hold on us. We can question the automatic judgments we make about ourselves and others, the narratives we construct about what we see, and the meanings we assign to our experiences.

This isn't to say that everything is an illusion or that no objective reality exists. Rather, it's an invitation to hold our perceptions more lightly, to remember that they are translations rather than direct experiences of reality. With this awareness comes greater freedom—freedom from rigid judgments, from harmful comparisons, and from the unnecessary suffering that arises when we mistake our perceptions for absolute truth.

OUR LYING EYES

THE NEUROSCIENCE OF VISUAL ILLUSIONS

Visual illusions are not just entertaining curiosities; they're windows into how our visual system works. By studying how and why our perception can be tricked, neuroscientists have gained valuable insights into the mechanisms underlying vision.

The Hermann Grid: Ghostly Dots

The Hermann grid illusion is named after the German physiologist Ludimar Hermann, who first described it in 1870. While studying visual perception, Hermann noticed that when people look at a grid of black squares separated by white lines, they often perceive illusory grey spots at the intersections—except at the point where their eyes are directly focused. This visual phenomenon became known as the *Hermann grid illusion* in his honor.

Look at the Hermann grid, and you'll notice ghostly gray dots appearing at the intersections of the white lines. But when you look directly at a specific intersection, the dot disappears. These dots aren't present in the image; they're created by a process in your retina called *lateral inhibition.*

YOUR MIND: TRANSLATED

The Herman grid illusion

Lateral inhibition enhances the contrast at boundaries between light and dark areas, helping us detect edges in the visual world. In the Hermann Grid, this process creates the illusion of gray dots at the intersections when viewed in your peripheral vision. It reminds us that even at the earliest stages of visual processing, our nervous system is actively modifying what we see.

The Kanizsa Triangle: Seeing What Isn't There

The Kanizsa triangle

The Kanizsa Triangle illusion (named after Italian psychologist Gaetano Kanizsa) shows how our visual system actively constructs perceptions rather than passively recording what's there. In this image, we perceive a white triangle that doesn't physically exist, formed by the arrangement of Pac-Man-like shapes. Our brains automatically complete the contours of the triangle, even though they're not present in the actual image.[23]

This phenomenon, known as *illusory contours*, demonstrates our brain's tendency to fill in missing information and perceive complete objects, even when portions are absent or occluded. It's an adaptive feature that helps us recognize partially hidden objects in our environment, but it also reveals something deeper: Our visual experience is not a passive reception of reality—it's an active construction.

And this active construction doesn't stop at vision. Our minds constantly fill in gaps in relationships, conversations, and even identities. We assume intentions behind a glance, imagine motives from a message, or judge someone's character based on a single interaction. Just as we see a triangle where none exists, we build stories from fragments—stories that feel complete but may not reflect the whole truth.

If perception is a construction, then so is much of what we think we "know." The people we envy, fear, or idealize may be illusions formed by selective impressions, much like the white triangle in the Kanizsa illusion. Understanding this can soften our judgments of others and of ourselves.

This awareness encourages us to pause and question what we perceive. Can we hold our assumptions lightly? Can we stay curious rather than conclusive? The mind's need for closure is strong, but clarity often comes not from rushing to complete the picture—but from learning to sit with what's incomplete.

In everyday life, this insight helps us listen better, observe more carefully, and live with a gentler grasp on our interpretations. It reminds us that behind every perception lies a process—not a mirror, but a lens. And that lens is ours to examine.

THE CULTURAL LENS OF VISION

Our cultural background, language, and experience profoundly influence how we see the world, often in ways we don't realize. Different cultures perceive visual information differently.

The Müller-Lyer Illusion Across Cultures

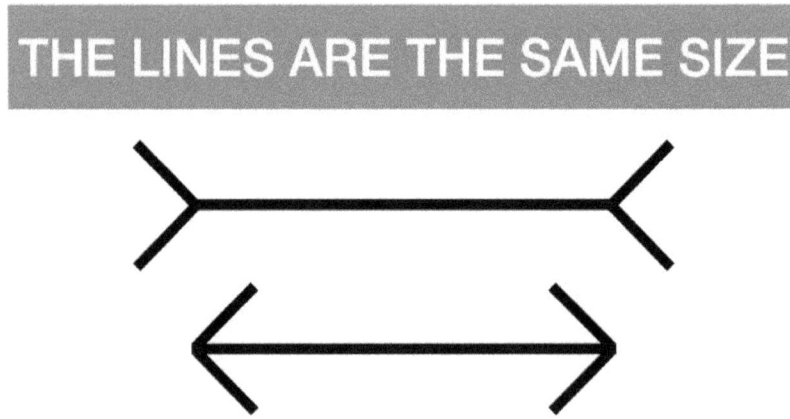

The Müller-Lyer illusion

The Müller-Lyer illusion consists of two lines of equal length, one with arrow-like fins pointing inward, the other with fins pointing outward. In Western cultures, people typically perceive the line with outward-pointing fins as longer than the one with inward-pointing fins, despite their identical length.

Interestingly, this illusion is much less pronounced in people from cultures with less exposure to carpentered environments (buildings with right angles and straight lines). For example, the San people of the Kalahari, who traditionally live in a non-carpentered environment, are much less susceptible to this illusion.[24] Our perceptual systems are shaped by our visual environment and experiences, literally changing how we see lines and angles.

Color Perception and Language

Languages differ in how they categorize colors, and these linguistic differences can influence color perception. For example, the Himba people of Namibia have fewer terms for color than English speakers but can distinguish between shades of green that look identical to most Westerners.[25]

In a famous study, researchers found that Russian speakers, who have different words for light blue (*goluboy*) and dark blue (*siniy*), could distinguish between these shades more quickly than English speakers, who use a single term "blue" for both.[26] The results of this study suggest that the language we speak can affect our visual perception at a fundamental level.

The Direction of Reading and Visual Attention

The direction in which we read—left-to-right in English, right-to-left in Arabic and Hebrew—influences how we scan visual scenes and perceive motion. People from cultures with left-to-right writing systems tend to scan scenes from left to right and perceive ambiguous motion as moving leftward, while those from right-to-left writing cultures show the opposite pattern.[27]

This effect extends to aesthetic judgments and spatial composition. Western artists tend to place the focal point of paintings slightly to the left of center, while Middle Eastern artists often place it to the right, reflecting their different reading directions.[28]

These cultural differences in visual perception remind us that what we consider "natural" or "obvious" ways of seeing the world are often the product of specific cultural conditioning and experience. Our eyes don't simply record the world; they interpret it through lenses shaped by our language, environment, and cultural background.

PRACTICE: CHALLENGING YOUR PERCEPTIONS

Today, choose one familiar object in your home and examine it as if you're seeing it for the first time. Notice its colors, textures, and details without immediately labeling it. How many aspects of this object have you overlooked before?

This exercise can help you recognize how quickly your mind categorizes and potentially oversimplifies your perceptions.

The next time you look at a loved one's face or gaze at a beautiful sunset, remember—you're not seeing reality. You're seeing your brain's carefully constructed version of reality, a translation so convincing you've never thought to question it.

> "Reality is merely an illusion, albeit a very persistent one."
> **— Albert Einstein**[29]

As we close this chapter, consider how profoundly your visual perceptions shape your understanding of the world. Your eyes don't simply record reality like a camera; they actively construct what you see based on a complex interplay of physical, psychological, and cultural factors.

The duck-rabbit illusion, the blind spot experiment, and the cultural variations in visual perception all point to a startling truth: What you see is not simply what is there but rather what your brain creates. Your visual experience is a translation of reality, filtered through the lens of your evolutionary heritage, personal history, and cultural background.

This understanding can be unsettling. If you can't trust your own eyes, what can you trust? But it can also be liberating.

By recognizing the constructed nature of perception, you gain the freedom to question your automatic interpretations and open yourself to new ways of seeing.

In the next chapter, we'll explore how a similar process of translation affects your auditory experience. If your eyes can deceive you, can your ears deceive you, too? As you'll discover, the words and sounds that shape your understanding of the world may be just as malleable as what you see.

CHAPTER THREE

OUR DEAF EARS

"We hear only what we understand."
— Johann Wolfgang von Goethe [1]

Close your eyes for a moment and listen. Really listen. What do you hear? The hum of an air conditioner? Birds outside your window? The sound of your own breathing? Traffic in the distance? Now ask yourself: Are you hearing everything that's actually there, or is your mind selecting, filtering, and interpreting these sounds?

Just as our eyes don't simply record visual information but actively construct what we see, our ears and auditory processing systems don't simply record sounds but actively shape what we hear. Our auditory experience, like our visual experience, is a translation of reality rather than a direct representation of it.

WHEN WORDS TRIGGER EMOTIONS: THE POWER OF ASSOCIATION

During my travels through the Caucasus Region and Central Asia, I observed a fascinating interplay between cultural context and ingrained biases in my own mind. Whenever a Muslim individual greeted me with the traditional Arabic phrase "As-Salaam-Alaikum," my body would react with a surge of anxiety. This visceral response stemmed from the Western media's portrayal of Islam as a religion of danger, violence, and conflict.

However, a moment of mindful reflection revealed the absurdity of this reaction. "As-Salaam-Alaikum" translates to "Peace be upon you"—a benevolent expression with no inherent threat. My initial anxiety was not a rational response to the present interaction but rather a conditioned reflex triggered by a subconscious association with negative connotations. This experience highlights the potent influence of media representation in shaping our perceptions and emotional responses, even when those representations contradict the reality on the ground.

Emotional Hijacking

Neuroscientist Joseph LeDoux coined the term *emotional hijacking* for the process by which our amygdala—a small, almond-shaped structure deep in our brain responsible for processing emotions—responds to stimuli before our conscious mind has a chance to evaluate them .[2] Once an emotional association is formed, it can be triggered automatically, bypassing rational thought.

Think about certain songs that instantly transport you to specific moments in your past. Perhaps a particular melody brings back memories of your first love, complete with the emotional resonance of that time. Or maybe a certain voice reminds you of a difficult period in your life, causing discomfort even inentirely different contexts. These reactions happen faster than conscious thought, illustrating how deeply our auditory processing is intertwined with our emotional systems. Psychologists call this effect "priming"— exposure to one stimulus influences our response to a subsequent stimulus, often without our awareness.[3]

The Power of Priming

In a classic experiment, participants who were exposed to words related to the elderly (such as "Florida," "bingo," and "retired") subsequently walked more slowly down the hallway when leaving the experiment than those exposed to neutral words. Remarkably, the participants had no awareness that their behavior had been influenced.[4]

Similarly, the sounds we hear can prime our subsequent perceptions and behaviors. Background music in shopping malls is carefully selected to influence consumer behavior. Fast-tempo music tends to make shoppers move more quickly through the store, while slow-tempo music encourages them to linger and potentially purchase more.5 Shoppers rarely notice this influence, yet their behavior changes measurably.

The Framing Effect

The power of priming is further illustrated by the framing effect, a cognitive bias in which people react differently to the same information depending on how it is presented. For instance, individuals are more likely to feel reassured by a 95% survival rate for scuba diving or heart surgery than by the equivalent statistic that 5 out of 100 people die during these activities. Despite conveying identical information, the positive framing elicits a more favorable response. Our brains, it seems, have a tendency to gravitate towards interpretations that align with our pre-existing beliefs and expectations.

Princeton University psychologist Daniel Kahneman and his colleague Amos Tversky demonstrated this principle in a famous experiment involving a hypothetical disease outbreak.6 When treatment options were framed in terms of lives saved, participants preferred the option that guaranteed saving 200 out of 600 people over the option offering a one-third probability of saving all 600 people. But when the identical options were framed in terms of deaths, preferences reversed. The information was mathematically equivalent, but the emotional response to different wording led to dramatically different preferences.

This selective filtering of information is not unique to humans. We observe similar phenomena in the animal kingdom. For example, turkey hens rely on the characteristic "cheeping" sound of their chicks to trigger maternal instincts. If they cannot hear this auditory cue, they may kill their own offspring.

Remarkably, a stuffed polecat, a natural predator of turkeys, can elicit brooding behavior from a hen if it emits the recorded "cheeping" sound, demonstrating the power of innate triggers and the potential for misinterpretation when those triggers are presented in an unexpected context.

These examples underscore the complex interplay of cognitive biases, social conditioning, and cultural influences in shaping our perceptions and behaviors. Our minds are not objective observers of reality but rather active interpreters, constantly filtering and framing information to fit within pre-existing mental models. Understanding these cognitive processes is crucial for cultivating critical thinking skills and navigating the complexities of a diverse and interconnected world.

AUDITORY ILLUSIONS AND CONTEXT

Our sense of hearing is a powerful tool that enables us to navigate the world, communicate, and connect with others. However, it is also susceptible to various forms of deception and distortion, which can lead to misunderstandings and misinterpretations of our environment.

The McGurk Effect: When Eyes Override Ears

Auditory illusions are one of the most intriguing aspects of our hearing. These sounds can be perceived differently depending on the listener's expectations, experiences, or even the context in which they are heard. A well-known example is the *McGurk effect*, first described in 1976 by psychologists Harry McGurk and John MacDonald in their paper "Hearing Lips and Seeing Voices." In the McGurk effect, conflicting visual and auditory stimuli lead to a misinterpretation of spoken words. For instance, when a person says "ba" while their lip movements resemble "ga," the listener may hear "da." This example highlights how our brain integrates sensory information, often prioritizing visual input over auditory data, leading to an altered perception of sound.7

The McGurk effect demonstrates that what we "hear" is actually a construction of our brain, integrating information from multiple senses. It's not just about the sound waves entering our ears but about how our brain interprets these signals in the context of other sensory information.

Phantom Words: Finding Patterns in Noise

Another fascinating auditory illusion is the phenomenon of phantom words. When exposed to a repeated loop of meaningless sounds or syllables, our brains often begin to perceive words and phrases that aren't actually there. Psychologist Diana Deutsch demonstrated this phenomenon with her speech-to-song illusion, in which a spoken phrase repeated several times begins to sound like it's being sung rather than spoken.[8]

These illusions occur because our brains are pattern-seeking organs, constantly trying to find meaning and structure in the sensory input we receive. When faced with ambiguous or repetitive auditory stimuli, our brains impose patterns based on our expectations, linguistic background, and experiences.

The Cocktail Party Effect

Have you ever noticed that you can suddenly hear your name mentioned across a crowded, noisy room? This phenomenon, known as the *cocktail party effect*, illustrates our brain's remarkable ability to filter and focus auditory attention.[9] Even in environments filled with multiple conversations and background noise, we can selectively attend to specific sounds that are personally relevant or important.

This selective attention is both a strength and a limitation of our auditory processing. It allows us to focus on important information in noisy environments, but it also means we miss much of what's happening around us. When we focus on one conversation, we often have little awareness of other nearby discussions, even though they're clearly audible. Our brains are not recording everything and then selecting what to focus on; instead, they're actively filtering in real time, constructing a limited auditory experience from the wealth of available sound information.

Context and Interpretation

Our perception of sound is also influenced by the volume and distance of the source. For example, sounds that are louder are often perceived as closer than they actually are. Conversely, softer sounds may be interpreted as farther away. These perceptions can lead to misjudgments about the location and proximity of objects or events. For instance, if you hear a siren in the distance, the volume may suggest it is closer than it truly is, potentially causing you to react inappropriately or with unnecessary urgency.

Context shapes our interpretation of sounds in profound ways. The same exact sound can be perceived differently depending on our expectations and the surrounding environment. In a striking experiment, researchers had participants listen to identical audio recordings in different contexts. When told they were hearing a religious service, participants reported hearing more distinct speech and positive emotions than when told they were hearing a political rally.10 The actual audio hadn't changed—only the listeners' expectations had.

THE DECEPTIVE NATURE OF HEARING

Background noise can also significantly affect how we perceive sounds. In noisy environments, such as crowded places or busy streets, distinguishing between different sounds becomes challenging, which can lead to misinterpretations of conversations or the inability to hear important auditory signals, such as warnings or alerts. The brain's ability to filter out background noise allows us to focus on specific sounds, but this ability is not foolproof. Sometimes our attention is drawn to irrelevant noise, causing us to miss critical information.

Linguistic Relativity in Sound Perception

The language we speak profoundly influences how we perceive and categorize sounds. Languages differ in their *phonemic inventories*—that is, the basic sound units that are recognized as distinct by speakers of the language. For example, Japanese speakers have difficulty distinguishing between the English "r" and "l" sounds because these are not separate phonemes in Japanese.11

This influence goes beyond simply recognizing individual sounds. It also affects how we mentally group and separate them. Rather than perceiving speech sounds as part of a continuous stream, we tend to interpret them as falling into discrete categories—a phenomenon known as *categorical perception*. For instance, when English speakers hear a range of sounds that gradually shift from /b/ to /p/, they don't hear a gradual change. Instead, they perceive a sharp boundary: one moment it's clearly /b/, and the next, it suddenly becomes /p/.

This boundary exists not because of the acoustic signal itself, but because of the phonemic categories built into the listener's native language. In other words, our brains are trained by our language to ignore subtle variations within a category and focus only on what makes one sound distinct from another sound in our language. This helps explain why sounds that seem very different to speakers of one language may sound practically identical to speakers of another.

By about six months of age, infants begin to lose the ability to distinguish between sound contrasts that don't exist in their native language, while maintaining or improving their ability to distinguish contrasts that are linguistically relevant.12

This means that speakers of different languages literally hear the world differently. What sounds like two distinct words to an English speaker might sound like the same word to a speaker of another language, and vice versa. Our auditory experience is fundamentally shaped by the language we learned as children.

The Link Between Hearing and Emotion

Our emotional state can greatly influence how we interpret sounds. For instance, fear or anxiety can heighten our sensitivity to certain noises, making us perceive them as more threatening than they actually are. Conversely, positive emotions can create a more favorable interpretation of sounds, leading us to find joy or comfort in them. This interplay between emotion and perception demonstrates how our mental and emotional states can shape our auditory experiences, often distorting reality in the process.

Research on individuals with anxiety disorders has shown that they tend to perceive neutral or ambiguous sounds as more threatening than those without anxiety.13 Someone with social anxiety might interpret a laugh in the distance as mockery directed at them, while someone without anxiety might assume it's unrelated to them.

Even our physical state affects sound perception. When we're tired, sounds can seem louder and more irritating. When we're hungry, food-related sounds like sizzling or crunching can become more salient and appealing.14 These effects remind us that our auditory experience isn't simply a recording of external sounds but rather an interpretation heavily influenced by our internal state.

Tinnitus and Internal Perception

Some individuals experience tinnitus, a perceived ringing, buzzing, or other sound without an external source. This condition highlights how our auditory system can generate sounds internally, leading to confusion and distress. People with tinnitus may struggle to differentiate between real sounds and those produced by their own minds, illustrating a profound disconnect between perception and reality.

The Prevalence of Tinnitus and Other Phantom Sounds

Tinnitus affects approximately 15-20% of people, with about 2% experiencing severe cases that interfere with daily life.15 For those with chronic tinnitus, the constant presence of sound that others can't hear creates a profound challenge to their understanding of reality. "Is this sound real?" becomes a question without a simple answer.

Beyond tinnitus, other forms of phantom sounds exist. *Musical ear syndrome* causes people to hear music that isn't playing. Auditory hallucinations associated with conditions like schizophrenia can include hearing voices or other complex sounds with no external source.16 These phenomena reveal how our auditory experience can be generated entirely within our minds, independent of external stimuli.

The Role of Expectation in Hearing

Even in healthy individuals, expectation plays a crucial role in what is heard. If we expect to hear a particular sound, we're more likely to perceive it, even when it's absent or ambiguous. This phenomenon is the basis for the *phonemic restoration effect*, where listeners "hear" sounds that have been replaced by noise in a recording because they expect those sounds to be there based on context.17

For example, if you hear "The **** is on the table" with a cough obscuring one word, you might "hear" the word "book" or "plate" depending on your expectations, even though no such word was actually present in the audio. Your brain fills in the missing information based on context and prior knowledge.

This automatic filling-in process usually serves us well, helping us understand speech in noisy environments. But it also means that what we think we hear isn't always what was actually said, especially in ambiguous or noisy situations. Our auditory experience is continuously shaped by our expectations and prior knowledge.

THE SOUND OF LANGUAGE AND THOUGHT

> "The limits of my language mean the limits of my world."
> **— Ludwig Wittgenstein**[18]

The relationship between language, sound, and thought runs deeper than we might realize. The words we hear and use don't just communicate ideas; they shape how we think and what we're capable of thinking.

How Language Shapes Thought

The *Sapir-Whorf hypothesis* suggests that the language we speak influences our thoughts and perceptions.[19] While the strong version of this hypothesis (that language determines thought) has been largely rejected, evidence supports a weaker version: Language shapes thought in subtle but significant ways.

For example, languages differ in how they represent time. English speakers tend to think of time linearly, moving from left to right, while Mandarin speakers more often conceptualize time as vertical, with the past above and the future below[20]. These differences correspond to how time is spoken about in these languages and influence how speakers think about temporal relationships.

These effects extend to auditory perception. The sounds of our native language literally shape what we hear. Russian speakers, who have distinct words for light blue (*goluboy*) and dark blue (*siniy*), can distinguish between these shades more quickly than English speakers can,[21] suggesting that the linguistic categories available to us affect not just how we label our perceptions but also the perceptions themselves.

The Inner Voice: Thought as Internal Speech

Many people experience inner speech—the sensation of "hearing" your own thoughts as if spoken internally. This phenomenon, studied extensively by psychologist Lev Vygotsky, suggests that our thinking processes are intimately connected with language.[22] For many of us, to think is to engage in a kind of internal dialogue, using the sounds and structures of language even when no one is speaking.

This inner voice isn't just a side effect of thought; it actively shapes our thinking. When people are prevented from using inner speech (by being asked to repeat meaningless sounds while thinking), their problem-solving abilities are often impaired, especially for complex tasks.[23] The sounds of language, even when only "heard" internally, provide a structure for our thoughts.

Yet not everyone experiences inner speech in the same way. Some people report thinking primarily in images, feelings, or abstract concepts rather than words.[24] This diversity in thought processes reminds us that while language and its sounds profoundly influence cognition, the relationship between language, sound, and thought varies significantly across individuals.

THE SOUNDSCAPE OF MODERN LIFE

Our modern world is filled with sounds that our ancestors never experienced: the ping of text messages, the hum of refrigerators, the roar of jet engines. These sounds have changed not just what we hear but also how we listen and respond to our environment.

Noise Pollution and Selective Hearing

The constant background noise of contemporary life—particularly in urban environments—has led many of us to develop a kind of selective deafness as a coping mechanism. We tune out the hum of air conditioners, the distant sound of traffic, and the chatter of colleagues in open-plan offices in order to focus on what's immediately relevant.[25]

This adaptive strategy helps us function in noisy environments, but it comes at a cost. We become less attuned to our auditory surroundings, less likely to notice subtle changes in our environment, and potentially less connected to the natural world. Studies have shown that exposure to natural soundscapes—birdsong, rushing water, rustling leaves—can reduce stress and improve cognitive function.[26] Yet many of us have learned to ignore these beneficial sounds along with the less desirable ones.

The Attention Economy of Sound

In our information-saturated world, sounds compete for our attention. Notification sounds are carefully designed to be both noticeable and emotionally neutral enough to avoid causing distress when heard repeatedly.[27] Advertisers use distinctive audio signatures to create brand recognition. Politicians and public speakers modulate their voices to convey authority and trustworthiness.

All of these intentionally designed sounds seek to influence not just what we hear but how we feel and behave in response. Our auditory environment has become increasingly engineered to elicit specific responses, often without our conscious awareness. This "attention economy" of sound represents a new frontier in how external forces shape our auditory experiences.

Our Musical Brain

Music offers perhaps the most striking example of how our auditory experience is constructed rather than simply received. What we hear as a beautiful melody, another person might hear as unremarkable or even unpleasant. Our response to music is shaped by cultural exposure, personal history, and even genetic factors.[28]

Cultural Variation in Music Perception

Different musical traditions use different scales, rhythmic patterns, and harmonic structures. Western music typically uses a 12-tone equal temperament scale, while traditional Indian music uses a 22-tone system, and Indonesian gamelan music uses scales that would sound "out of tune" to Western ears.[29]

Listeners raised in these different traditions develop distinct expectations and preferences. What sounds "natural" or "correct" to one listener may sound strange or discordant to another. These differences aren't just matters of preference; they reflect fundamental differences in how listeners parse and interpret the same auditory input.

Even within cultures, musical preferences vary widely and can be deeply tied to identity. The music we love becomes part of who we are, influencing how we dress, whom we socialize with, and even our political views.[30] Few other forms of sound have such profound effects on our sense of self and belonging.

The Emotional Power of Music

Music's ability to evoke emotions is unparalleled among auditory experiences. Certain musical passages can reliably induce feelings of joy, sadness, tension, or relaxation across listeners.[31] This emotional response isn't just psychological; it's also physiological. Music can lower cortisol levels, increase dopamine release, and even synchronize breathing and heart rates among listeners.[32]

What makes music so emotionally powerful? One theory suggests that music creates emotional effects through the building and release of tension—setting up expectations and then either fulfilling them (creating satisfaction) or violating them (creating surprise)[33]. In this view, what we hear in music isn't just sound but a complex narrative of tension and resolution that engages emotional processing.

This emotional engagement with music illustrates how deeply interpretive our auditory experience is. We don't just hear the notes; we hear anticipation, resolution, joy, or melancholy. The same sequence of sounds can evoke entirely different emotional responses depending on cultural background, personal associations, and current mood—further evidence that what we hear is never simply a recording of external reality but rather an active construction of meaning.

THE PHONOLOGICAL LOOP AND MEMORY

Our ability to remember what we hear is facilitated by what psychologists call the *phonological loop*—a component of working memory that temporarily stores and rehearses verbal information.[34] This mental system allows us to hold a phone number in mind while dialing or follow a conversation by keeping earlier words in memory while processing later ones.

The phonological loop has limited capacity, typically allowing us to remember about seven items (plus or minus two) for a short period.[35] This limitation affects not just what we remember but also what we perceive. When listening to complex or rapid speech, we may miss elements that exceed our working memory capacity, even though the sounds physically entered our ears.

This memory system also influences how we interpret ambiguous sounds. When we can't clearly hear a word, our brains attempt to match the partial information with words stored in memory. The words we've heard recently or frequently are more likely to be selected as matches, creating potential misunderstandings based not on what was said but on what we expected to hear.[36]

Our sense of hearing is essential for interaction and communication, but it is not infallible. The various ways in which it can deceive us—through auditory illusions, cultural influences, background noise, emotional states, and even internal perceptions—remind us of the complexities of sensory interpretation. By understanding these limitations, we can cultivate a more critical approach to our auditory experiences, fostering a deeper awareness of how our perceptions can be shaped and sometimes misled. This awareness can enhance our communication skills, improve our relationships, and help us navigate the world with greater clarity.

PRACTICE: MINDFUL LISTENING

Set aside five minutes today for a mindful listening exercise. Find a comfortable position, close your eyes, and simply listen to the sounds around you without judging or categorizing them. Notice how many layers of sound exist simultaneously. Can you detect sounds you normally filter out? This practice can heighten your awareness of how selectively your brain processes auditory information.

OUR DEAF EARS

Consider this unsettling thought: Your mind doesn't just translate what you hear—it actively creates much of what you think you're hearing. The voices of loved ones, the music that moves you to tears, the whispered secrets that change your life ... how much of what you "hear" is actually your mind's invention?

> "We don't hear with our ears, we hear with our brain."
> —Seth S. Horowitz[37]

As we conclude this chapter, reflect on how your auditory experience, like your visual experience, is not a faithful recording of objective reality but an interpretation—a translation shaped by your expectations, emotions, cultural background, and personal history.

The words that move you, the sounds that startle you, the music that transports you—all are experienced through your mind's interpretive processes. What you hear is not simply what is "out there" but a complex construction created through the interaction of external stimuli and internal processes.

This understanding can be both humbling and empowering. It is humbling because it reminds us that our perceptions are limited and sometimes misleading. It is empowering because awareness of these limitations opens the possibility of more conscious and critical listening.

In the next chapter, we explore how this process of translation extends to all our senses and how they work together to create our overall experience of reality. If both vision and hearing involve such complex interpretation, what about touch, taste, and smell? And how does the brain integrate all these translated sensory experiences into a coherent understanding of the world?

CHAPTER FOUR

OUR SENSES/THE SENSES

"There is nothing in the intellect that was not first in the senses."
— Thomas Aquinas[1]

When you bite into an apple, what do you experience? The crisp crunch as your teeth break through the skin, the sweet-tart flavor spreading across your tongue? The smooth surface against your fingertips, the fresh scent wafting to your nose, the bright red or green color that caught your eye in the first place? This seemingly simple experience involves all five of your traditional senses—touch, taste, smell, hearing, and sight—working together to create what you perceive as "eating an apple."

But is your experience of this apple the same as mine? Is the sweetness you taste identical to the sweetness I taste? Is your perception of its red color the same as my perception of red?

These questions lead us into the fascinating territory of sensory perception and the complex relationship between our sensory organs, our brains, and our subjective experience of reality.

THE OBSERVER'S PARADOX

The great difficulty in studying the human mind is that we, the observers, are humans ourselves. Our brains, which are an instrument of study, are simultaneously the object of that study. We are surrounded by human beings all our lives, with the result that we take society and all that it imprints on us for granted. It is all but impossible to speculate about that which seems so natural—to view it from a different and unbiased angle, to climb out of our own bodies, and to become strangers to ourselves.

The Challenge of Self-Observation

The observer's paradox was articulated by the philosopher Edmund Husserl, who noted that to study consciousness, we must use consciousness itself as our tool.[2] A good analogy is trying to see your own eye without a mirror—the very organ of sight cannot directly observe itself. Similarly, our mind cannot step outside itself objectively to study how it works. As Neuroscientist V. S. Ramachandran notes, "The contents of consciousness are trying to grab hold of the processes that gave rise to them,"[3] creating a fundamental limitation in how we can understand our own perceptual processes.

Think about it this way: When you observe anything, you're not just seeing the thing itself; you're seeing your perception of the thing, filtered through your sensory apparatus and interpreted by your brain. To study perception, then, is to study the filter through which we must look to conduct the study—a circular challenge that has puzzled philosophers and scientists for centuries.

The Limits of Introspection

Introspection—looking inward at our own mental processes—was once considered the primary method for understanding the mind. However, as psychologist William James noted, introspection is itself a form of observation subject to the same biases and limitations as any other form of perception.[4] The moment we try to observe our own thought processes, we change those very processes.

Consider what happens when you try to observe yourself falling asleep. The very act of monitoring yourself prevents the sleep you're trying to observe. Similarly, trying to observe your own sensory processing in action changes the experience you're trying to understand.

This doesn't mean introspection is worthless—far from it. But it does mean we need to approach our understanding of perception with humility, recognizing that our view from inside the system will always be partial and potentially biased.

The Social Construction of Perception

All human behavior is acquired, and we can therefore be molded by upbringing and education. It only takes a couple tweaks here and there to create a mentally healthy child who will become loving and caring to others, or a traumatic experience that will affect that child's behavior for life. A traumatized child might project their pain onto others as a way of finding peace or use a defense mechanism to protect themselves from something that happened 20 years ago. The mind, not being able to recognize whether the thoughts we're having are current or from the past, produces the same feelings and reactions regardless.

Our sensory experiences are not just biological events but are deeply shaped by social and cultural factors. Anthropologist Clifford Geertz argued that even our most basic sensory experiences are filtered through cultural frameworks that give them meaning.[5] What tastes good or bad, what smells pleasant or unpleasant, what feels comfortable or uncomfortable—all are influenced by cultural norms and personal history.

Consider how different cultures have radically different concepts of personal space and acceptable physical contact. In Mediterranean cultures, close physical proximity and frequent touching during conversation may be normal, while in Northern European cultures, greater physical distance is typically maintained.[6] These cultural differences become ingrained in our sensory experience so deeply that violations of these norms can produce genuine physical discomfort—a visceral sense that something is "wrong" when someone stands "too close" according to our cultural conditioning.

MEMORY AND SENSORY EXPERIENCE

Memory is based on electrical oscillatory cycles that are interrupted by a particular stimulus—that is, by a specific experience. The ability to imitate others is found only in the most intelligent learners and is far more evident in humans than in any other species.

How Memory Shapes Perception

Our sensory experiences are profoundly influenced by our memories. When you smell freshly baked bread and feel a sense of comfort, you aren't responding simply to the chemical compounds in the air—instead, your brain is connecting the current sensory input with positive memories associated with that smell. The neural pathways activated by the smell overlap with pathways associated with past experiences, creating a rich, emotionally textured perception.[7]

This memory-infused perception works across all your senses. The texture of a fabric against your skin might remind you of a beloved childhood blanket. A particular musical phrase might transport you to the first time you heard that song. These associations aren't just added onto pure sensory experiences—they're integral to the perception itself.

Neuroscientist Antonio Damasio describes how our brains are constantly creating "somatic markers"—emotional memories attached to sensory experiences that guide our future interactions with similar stimuli.[8] These markers help us navigate the world efficiently, but they also mean that no sensory experience is ever truly "raw" or unfiltered by past experience.

The Constructive Nature of Memory

Importantly, memory itself is not a faithful recording but a construction. Each time we recall a memory, we essentially recreate it, making it vulnerable to modification.[9] This reconstructive process means that our sensory memories—how something felt, tasted, smelled, looked, or sounded—can shift over time.

Think about a food you disliked as a child but enjoy as an adult. Has the food changed, or has your perception of it changed? Likely both. This change in perception involves a modification of sensory memory—your brain has literally rewritten how it remembers that taste experience.

This malleable quality of sensory memory means that our current perceptions are influenced by past experiences, but they can also retroactively alter how we remember those past experiences, creating a complex, dynamic relationship between memory and perception.

The Imitative Urge

The imitative urge is a form of instinctive behavior that developed fully only in *Homo sapiens* and influences us very decisively. This instinct is the source of incentive ambition, envy and dislike. The knowledge that other people possess abilities or artificial organs that we lack but find desirable frustrates our imitative urge and causes feelings of discontent. The desire to imitate presupposes an ability to visualize oneself with someone else's qualities and is thus linked with mental activity. We cannot aspire to possess that which we are incapable of imagining.

Mirror Neurons and Embodied Simulation

The neurological basis for our imitative capacity lies partly in what neuroscientists call *mirror neurons*—cells that fire both when we perform an action and when we observe someone else performing the same action.[10] This neural mirroring allows us to internally simulate others' experiences, creating a kind of sensory empathy.

When you watch someone bite into a lemon and wince, you might feel a sympathetic pucker in your own mouth. When you see someone touch a hot stove and recoil in pain, you might feel a flash of discomfort in your own hand. These are not just sympathetic reactions but actual embodied simulations—your brain is partially activating the same sensory circuits that would fire if you were having the experience yourself.[11]

This capacity for embodied simulation helps explain why watching movies or reading books can create such vivid sensory experiences. When an author describes the taste of rich chocolate cake in vivid detail, your brain activates many of the same neural pathways that would activate if you were actually eating the cake. Your sensory experience extends beyond your immediate environment through this remarkable capacity for simulation.

Social Learning Through Sensory Pathways

Our imitative capacity transforms how we learn. Humans can acquire new skills not just through trial and error but also through observation and sensory simulation. When you watch an expert musician play, your brain is not just processing visual and auditory information—it's creating a kind of sensory template for your own eventual performance.[12] At its core, this phenomenon reveals that humans are fundamentally wired for collaborative learning. Observation becomes a form of participation, where mental engagement with another's performance creates genuine understanding and skill development. This capacity for imitation and simulation enables a profound form of empathetic learning that transcends mere copying or mimicking. When we watch an expert perform—whether playing an instrument, painting, or speaking—our brains create mental blueprints and engage in internal rehearsal, allowing us to learn more efficiently even before physically attempting the skill ourselves. Observation transforms from passive watching into active preparation for learning.

This sensory-based social learning gives humans an enormous evolutionary advantage, allowing for the rapid transmission of complex skills across generations. It's also the basis for cultural transmission of sensory preferences and aversions. Children learn which foods should taste good, which sounds are pleasant or unpleasant, and which physical sensations are normal or concerning largely through observing others' sensory reactions.

Top-Down versus Bottom-Up Processing

Bottom-up processing refers to the fact that perceptions are built from sensory input. On the other hand, how we interpret those sensations is influenced by our available knowledge, our experiences, and our thoughts through a process called *top-down processing*.

While our sensory receptors (hearing, seeing, smelling, touching, tasting, and thinking) are constantly collecting information from the environment and the outside world, it is ultimately how our mind "interprets" that information that affects how we interact with the world and the people around us.

The Dance of Sensation and Expectation

To understand the interplay between bottom-up and top-down processing, consider what happens when you taste a familiar food. The bottom-up process involves taste receptors on your tongue detecting chemical compounds and sending signals to your brain. The top-down process involves your expectations about how the food should taste based on past experience, what you've been told about it, and even its appearance.

In a fascinating experiment, researchers gave participants wine to taste while they were in an fMRI machine that monitored brain activity. When told they were drinking an expensive wine (regardless of its actual price), participants not only reported enjoying it more but showed increased activity in the brain's pleasure centers compared to when they thought they were drinking cheap wine.[13] The same sensory input—the same wine molecules interacting with the same taste receptors—produced different neural and subjective experiences based on top-down expectations.

Perception as Prediction

Modern neuroscience suggests that perception is largely a predictive process. Rather than passively receiving sensory information, our brains actively generate predictions about what we expect to sense and then compare those predictions with actual sensory input.[14]

This predictive framework explains many perceptual phenomena. When you enter a dark room, your brain immediately begins generating predictions about the layout based on your memory of similar spaces and partial visual cues. As your eyes adjust and more visual information becomes available, your brain updates its predictions, creating the experience of the room gradually "appearing" as your vision adapts.

These predictions happen across all sensory modalities and operate largely outside conscious awareness. When you hear someone speaking, your brain is constantly predicting the next sounds based on your knowledge of language, the context of the conversation, and the speaker's habits. When those predictions are accurate, comprehension feels effortless. When they're repeatedly wrong—as when listening to someone with a strong unfamiliar accent—understanding requires more conscious effort as your predictive system recalibrates.[15]

SENSATION IS PHYSICAL, PERCEPTION IS PSYCHOLOGICAL

It is helpful to remember that sensation is a physical process, whereas perception is psychological. The senses never deceive humans, but sensory information can be misinterpreted. For example, upon walking into a kitchen and smelling the scent of baking cinnamon rolls, the sensation is the scent receptors detecting the odor of cinnamon, but the perception may be "Mmm, this smells like the bread Grandma used to bake when the family gathered for holidays." Your nose detected the scent, but your mind gave the scent its most emotionally significant meaning.

This distinction between sensation and perception explains why the same sensory experience can have radically different meanings for different people. The sound of fireworks might trigger joyful anticipation in one person, indifference in another, and terrifying flashbacks in someone with combat-related PTSD. The sensory input—the loud bang—is identical, but the perception varies dramatically based on each person's psychological framework and past experiences.

Sensory Adaptation

Although our perceptions are built from sensations, not all sensations result in perception. In fact, due to *sensory adaptation*, we often don't perceive stimuli that remain relatively constant over prolonged periods of time. Consider the fact that your nose is right in the middle of your field of vision—go ahead, look at it right now. You can see it, right? But do you see it all the time, even though it's always there? No, and the reason is that your mind filters out what it considers unnecessary information. Again, you don't do this consciously—your mind does it automatically. The fact that you no longer perceive your nose visually demonstrates sensory adaptation and shows that while sensation and perception are closely associated, they are different. In addition, according the theory of *inattentional amnesia*, many potential memories never form due to attention failure and thus become impossible to recall.

Sensory adaptation serves a crucial evolutionary function. By filtering out constant or predictable stimuli, our brains can remain alert to changes in our environment that might signal opportunity or danger. When you first put on a watch, you may be acutely aware of the sensation against your skin, but within minutes, this perception fades from your awareness. Your sensory receptors haven't stopped detecting the pressure; your brain has simply determined that this constant input provides no new information and doesn't require conscious attention.[16]

This adaptive filtering happens across all the senses. The constant hum of an air conditioner disappears from auditory awareness. The smell of your own home becomes imperceptible to you (though visitors can still detect it). Even the sensation of your clothes against your skin vanishes from your consciousness most of the time.

What's remarkable is the selectivity of this filtering. Your brain can tune out the sensation of your socks against your feet while remaining exquisitely sensitive to a tiny tickle that might indicate an insect crawling on your skin. This selective attention to potentially important sensory information while filtering out the constant background demonstrates the active, interpretive nature of perception.

Selective Attention and Inattentional Blindness

Here's a fun activity: Go to YouTube right now, type "Selective Attention Test" in the search bar, and see if you can count the passes. I bet you can't even make it to 6! After watching, come back here to continue reading.

The Invisible Gorilla Experiment

The "invisible gorilla" experiment, conducted by psychologists Christopher Chabris and Daniel Simons, dramatically illustrates the limitations of our attention.[17] In this famous study, participants were asked to watch a video of people passing basketballs and count the number of passes made by players wearing white shirts. During the video, a person in a gorilla suit walks through the scene, stops in the center, thumps their chest, and then walks off. Remarkably, about half of the viewers completely fail to notice the gorilla, even though it's in full view for several seconds.

The point of showing you this famous experiment is to demonstrate how "blind" the mind can be. Rather than focusing on every detail of any given situation, our minds—trying to be economical—concentrate on things they believe are most important. In doing so, they filter out everything else or "fill in the blanks" with what they think matters most. The brain is always trying to register and interpret things it believes will provide us with the most value, but in doing so, important visual information can sometimes get overlooked.

The Attentional Spotlight

Attention functions like a spotlight, illuminating certain aspects of our sensory experience while leaving others in darkness. This selective process is necessary because our brains have limited processing capacity. The amount of sensory information available at any moment far exceeds what our conscious mind can process.[18]

Consider what happens when you're having a conversation in a noisy restaurant. Your auditory system is receiving all the sounds in the environment—other conversations, kitchen noises, background music, traffic outside—but your attention spotlight focuses on the voice of your companion, elevating that sensory input to conscious awareness while relegating other sounds to the background.

This spotlight isn't fixed in size or intensity. It can broaden to take in an entire vista or narrow to focus on a tiny detail. It can intensify to capture subtle sensory information (like trying to hear a whisper) or relax to process more general impressions. And, crucially, it can shift rapidly from one focus to another, creating the illusion of simultaneous awareness of multiple streams of sensory information.[19]

Change Blindness

Related to inattentional blindness is the phenomenon of change blindness—our remarkable inability to notice even substantial changes in our visual field when those changes occur during disruptions to visual processing.[20]

In change blindness experiments, participants view two alternating images that are identical except for one significant difference. If the images alternate with a brief blank screen between them, people often require many viewings before noticing even major changes like the disappearance of a building or a shift in an object's color.

This phenomenon suggests that our visual perception is not a continuous, high-resolution recording of our environment but rather a series of snapshots that our brain stitches together into the illusion of a continuous experience. The details we think we perceive are often constructions based on previous views and expectations rather than active perceptions of what's currently in front of us.

Selective Deafness and Other Sensory Filtering

While the gorilla experiment demonstrates inattentional blindness, similar phenomena occur in other sensory modalities. *Inattentional deafness* is our failure to hear sounds that would normally be obvious. We do not hear those sounds because our attention is focused elsewhere.[21] For example, subway riders engrossed in their phones often fail to hear announcements, even at normal volume.

Even our sense of touch demonstrates selective attention. When deeply focused on a task, you might not notice physical sensations that would otherwise be obvious—a slight ache, the pressure of your chair, or even someone lightly touching your shoulder. It's not that the sensory information isn't reaching your brain; it's that the information is being filtered out before reaching your conscious awareness.

These phenomena remind us that our sensory experience is not comprehensive but highly selective. What we perceive is just a fraction of what our sensory organs detect, filtered through the lens of attention that prioritizes information deemed relevant to our current goals and concerns.

HOW EMOTIONS COLOR PERCEPTION

Our perceptions are distorted when we are hungry, sexually aroused, or frightened. In these states, we increasingly think exclusively of food, seek a mate, or feel overwhelmed by dangers and difficulties.

The Biological Basis of Emotional Perception

The neural pathways connecting our emotional centers to our sensory processing regions ensure that our perceptions are never emotionally neutral.[22] The amygdala, which processes emotional responses, has direct connections to all sensory processing areas of the brain and can modulate how sensory information is processed even before it reaches conscious awareness.

When you're afraid, your visual processing changes—you become more sensitive to peripheral movement and potential threats. When you're hungry, olfactory (smell) processing shifts to make food smells more salient. When you're in love, touch receptors become more sensitive to the physical contact from your beloved.[23] These perceptual shifts aren't conscious choices but rather automatic adjustments of your sensory systems based on your emotional state.

The Cognitive Influence of Emotion

Beyond these biological effects, emotions influence how we cognitively interpret sensory information. When anxious, we're more likely to interpret ambiguous sensory cues as threatening. A creaking floorboard at night becomes evidence of an intruder to an anxious mind, while a calm person might barely notice it or attribute it to the house settling.

Research shows that people in positive emotional states tend to process sensory information more globally and inclusively, taking in the "big picture," while negative emotions tend to narrow perceptual focus to specific details.[24] Thus you might fail to notice a beautiful sunset when you're upset about an argument but might be especially receptive to natural beauty when you're feeling content.

The Perpetuating Cycle of Emotional Perception

Emotional influences on perception are particularly powerful because they can create self-reinforcing cycles. When you're anxious, your perceptual systems become biased toward detecting threats, which leads to finding more evidence of potential danger, which further increases anxiety, which further biases perception, and so on.[25]

Understanding this cycle offers a key insight into how we can become trapped in emotional states. Depression doesn't just make you feel sad; it changes what you notice and how you interpret sensory information, creating a perceptual world that confirms and reinforces the depression. Breaking such cycles often requires interventions that address both the emotion itself and the perceptual biases it creates.

MORAL PERCEPTION AND INNATE REACTIONS

Our moral sense is tied to modes of reaction that are already innate in us. Certain situations elicit very specific reactions, whether we like it or not. The mistreatment of a child or the bullying of a defenseless person provokes a sense of outrage, whereas self-sacrifice on behalf of family, friends, or country tends to arouse our admiration.

The Moral Foundations of Sensory Reactions

Psychologist Jonathan Haidt argues that humans have innate moral intuitions that operate more like sensory perceptions than rational judgments.[26] We don't reason our way to feeling disgusted by certain behaviors or moved by acts of kindness—we feel these responses immediately, much as we feel pain when touching something hot.

These moral intuitions have sensory components. Moral disgust activates some of the same neural circuits as physical disgust—which is why we use phrases like "that leaves a bad taste in my mouth" to describe morally objectionable situations.[27] Similarly, witnessing acts of compassion can trigger physical sensations of warmth and opening in the chest—the physical components of the emotion of elevation.

These embodied moral responses suggest that our ethical sense is not separate from our sensory experience but rather deeply intertwined with it. When we say we "see" someone's goodness or "sense" their intentions, we're not speaking purely metaphorically, because moral perception has genuine sensory dimensions.

Cultural Variation in Moral Perception

While some basic moral perceptions appear universal, there's significant cultural variation in what triggers them. Different cultures have different "moral taste buds"—sensitivities to particular types of moral situations.[28] Some cultures are particularly attuned to violations of hierarchy or authority, while others are more sensitive to harm or fairness violations.

These cultural differences in moral perception can be as profound as differences in color categorization or phoneme distinction. Just as speakers of different languages literally hear speech sounds differently, people from different moral cultures may have fundamentally different perceptual experiences of the same social situations.

Understanding these variations helps explain why moral disagreements can be so intractable. When people from different moral cultures witness the same event, they don't just interpret it differently—they quite literally perceive different aspects of it through different moral lenses.

THE NAMING HABIT AND DIMINISHED CURIOSITY

The habit of quickly naming and categorizing things can sometimes diminish our curiosity, causing us to overlook the complexity and wonder that closer examination might reveal. When we recognize how much our language shapes our perception, we begin to see that our understanding of reality is filtered through mental frameworks that can both illuminate and limit what we notice.

The Double-Edged Sword of Categorization

Naming and categorization are essential cognitive tools. By grouping similar sensory experiences under a single label, we create conceptual shortcuts that allow us to navigate the world efficiently.[29] Recognizing that a furry, four-legged animal belongs to the category "dog" helps us predict its behavior and decide how to interact with it.

But this efficiency comes at a cost. Once we've named something, we often stop truly seeing it. Instead of perceiving its unique qualities in the present moment, we see only our mental category and the expectations that come with it. The philosopher Alan Watts described this experience as mistaking the menu for the meal—confusing our abstract concepts about things with the direct experience of the things themselves.[30]

This categorization process is automatic and largely unconscious. When you walk through a forest, you don't consciously decide to stop seeing individual trees and start seeing "forest." Instead, your perceptual system makes this shift automatically. The problem arises when these categories become rigid and prevent us from noticing details that don't fit our preconceptions.

Childlike Perception and the Loss of Wonder

Have you ever noticed that many young children are amazed by everything they encounter? They aren't able to identify these objects or experiences—they just live them without judgment or labels. That's why they believe that toys came to life and their little cars are really racing. Everything seems magical, and maybe shocking.

Developmental psychologists note that, unlike adults, young children have an ability to see things as they are, free from the accumulated layers of categorization and habitual response.[31] A child might spend an hour fascinated by the movement of ants or the texture of a stone because they're experiencing these things directly, without immediately placing them in mental boxes labeled "boring" or "ordinary."

This capacity for fresh perception doesn't completely disappear in adulthood but it does become increasingly rare, typically emerging only in moments of unusual mental states or deliberate practice such as meditation. The Zen concept of "beginner's mind" refers to this ability to perceive without preconception, to approach experience with the fresh curiosity of a child rather than the habitual responses of an adult.[32]

OUR SENSES/THE SENSES

Reclaiming Perceptual Freshness

We rarely experience awe in our daily lives, because we think we already know everything. We've become addicted to novelty, constantly scrolling through social media feeds where nothing captures our attention for more than a few seconds.

This constant quest for novelty paradoxically diminishes our capacity for genuine curiosity. When everything is reduced to a quick hit of newness, we lose the ability to deeply engage with any single perceptual experience. We see more but perceive less, constantly skimming the surface without diving into the depths.

Reclaiming the capacity for fresh perception requires intentionally slowing down and suspending our habitual categorization processes. Mindfulness meditation, drawing, or nature observation can help us temporarily step outside our naming habit and experience sensory input more directly.[33] By deliberately attending to the sensory qualities of ordinary experiences—the exact shade of blue in the sky, the complex flavor profile of a familiar food, the intricate pattern of a leaf—we can begin to restore the sense of wonder that comes with seeing things as if for the first time.

YOUR MIND: TRANSLATED

THE STOIC PERSPECTIVE ON PERCEPTION

Because our understanding of events and situations is filtered through our personal biases, experiences, and interpretations, we must remember to question and seek a deeper understanding rather than accept things at face value.

Stoicism emerged in ancient Greece around the 3rd century BCE and flourished through the Roman Empire until the 3rd century CE, with notable figures including founder Zeno of Citium in Athens, the freed slave philosopher Epictetus, and the Roman Emperor Marcus Aurelius. At its core, Stoicism taught that true happiness and peace come from focusing exclusively on what lies within our control—our thoughts, actions, and responses—while accepting what we cannot change. The Stoics believed that virtue, consisting of wisdom, justice, courage, and temperance, represents the only genuine good, far more valuable than external things such as wealth, fame, or pleasure. They emphasized living according to reason rather than being driven by emotions, practicing resilience in the face of life's inevitable challenges, and aligning oneself with the natural order of the universe. Their central philosophy can be summed up in the fundamental distinction between what is "up to you" and what is "not up to you." In other words, they advocated for a life of inner tranquility achieved through virtuous living regardless of external circumstances.

OUR SENSES/THE SENSES

The Stoic philosophers understood perception as an interpretation rather than a direct representation of reality. As Marcus Aurelius said, "Everything we hear is an opinion, not a fact. Everything we see is a perspective, not the truth." In distinguishing between opinion and fact, Marcus Aurelius wasn't suggesting that all perception is equally subjective or that no objective reality exists. Rather, he was highlighting the crucial difference between the raw sensory data we receive and the judgments we immediately attach to those data.[34]

For the Stoics, emotional suffering comes primarily from these automatic judgments rather than from sensory experiences themselves. It's not the sensation of pain that causes suffering but rather our judgment that the pain is terrible and shouldn't be happening. It's not the perception of someone's behavior that upsets us but our interpretation that their behavior is intentionally harmful or inappropriate.[35]

This distinction between sensation and judgment offers a powerful way to relate differently to challenging experiences. By recognizing that our interpretations are not intrinsic to the sensory experiences themselves, we gain the freedom to question those interpretations and potentially adopt different, less distressing ones.

Modern Applications of Stoic Perceptual Wisdom

Contemporary therapeutic approaches like cognitive behavioral therapy (CBT) build on the Stoics' insight about the relationship between perception and interpretation. CBT helps people identify automatic thoughts that accompany their perceptions and evaluate whether these thoughts are accurate or helpful.[36]

For instance, if you perceive a friend not returning your greeting (sensory input) and automatically think "They're ignoring me because they're angry with me" (interpretation), CBT would encourage you to examine that interpretation. Is it the only possible explanation? What evidence supports or contradicts it? Might there be other, equally plausible interpretations of the same perceptual experience?

This practice of separating perception from interpretation aligns precisely with the Stoic approach to navigating a world of potentially misleading appearances. By cultivating this discernment, we develop greater psychological flexibility and resilience in the face of challenging sensory experiences.

EMOTIONS AS GUIDES, NOT MASTERS

Emotions are central to the human experience, but they should not control us. One of the most valuable lessons that young people can learn is how to think critically about language—recognizing that words can mislead, manipulate, or oversimplify complex realities.

We need emotions and could not think without them, but they must be handled with the utmost caution. They restrict our freedom of thought and lead our wishes by the hand. Once a brain has employed certain concepts for twenty or thirty years, it is not in a position to part with them, and once they have propagated themselves for generations, they acquire the stability of a firmly rooted tree. The young and developing brain is still free and unrestricted.

Emotions as Perceptual Information

Contemporary emotion researchers view emotions not as irrational impulses that cloud judgment but as sophisticated information-processing systems that provide valuable data about our relationship to our environment.[37] When you feel fear, that emotion is giving you information about a potential threat. When you feel joy, that emotion is signaling opportunity or fulfillment. When you feel anger, that emotion is alerting you to a possible violation of your boundaries or values.

The problem arises not from having emotions but from treating emotional reactions as the final word on reality rather than as one source of information among many. Like other perceptual systems, emotional perception can be misleading. Just as optical illusions reveal the limitations of visual processing, emotional illusions can lead us astray when emotional responses are triggered by situations that resemble but don't actually present the conditions that those emotions evolved to detect.[38]

For example, the fear response that served our ancestors well when encountering predators can be maladaptive when triggered by public speaking or social disapproval. The disgust response that protected us from contaminated food can be misapplied to unfamiliar cultural practices. Recognizing these emotional misapplications requires developing a meta-awareness of our emotional reactions rather than simply accepting them as accurate reflections of reality.

The Role of Language in Emotional Perception

The labels we apply to our emotional experiences profoundly shape how we perceive and respond to those experiences. Psychologist Lisa Feldman Barrett argues that emotions are not hardwired, universal reactions but rather constructed experiences that vary significantly across cultures and individuals, with language playing a crucial role in this construction.[39]

Different languages carve up the emotional landscape in different ways. Portuguese has *saudade*, a specific type of longing with no direct English equivalent. German has *schadenfreude*, the pleasure derived from another's misfortune. Finnish has *sisu*, a concept of extraordinary determination in the face of extreme adversity. These linguistic differences don't just affect how people communicate about emotions; they influence how people subjectively experience emotions.

Even within a single language, the specific words we use to label our emotional experiences can alter those experiences. Describing yourself as "anxious" versus "excited" when experiencing the same physiological arousal can change how you feel and perform.[40] This linguistic reframing isn't just putting a positive spin on a negative experience—it can actually transform the subjective quality of the experience itself.

This malleability of emotional experience through language offers both caution and opportunity. We should be wary of uncritically accepting cultural or linguistic defaults for categorizing our emotional experiences. But we can also intentionally expand our emotional vocabulary, developing more nuanced ways of recognizing and describing our feelings, which in turn creates richer, more differentiated emotional experiences.

THE LIMITATIONS OF SENSORY KNOWLEDGE

Human reason is limited to the objects of sense experience; that is, it is impossible to see the world as it truly is from outside or beyond the senses. Even within the realm of experience, mistakes can occur because all sensory knowledge is ambiguous. A coil of rope can be mistaken for a snake, and vice versa. Furthermore, a person may be aware that what is seen, heard, or touched has the potential to deceive—but what if the entire process of acquiring information through the senses is itself an illusion?

Kant and the Phenomenal World

Philosopher Immanuel Kant argued that we can never know the "thing-in-itself" (the noumenon) but only the "thing-as-it-appears" (the phenomenon).41 According to Kant, space and time are not properties of the external world but rather structures imposed by our minds to organize sensory experience. Similarly, concepts like causality are not discovered in the world but brought to experience by our cognitive architecture.

This view suggests a profound limitation to human knowledge: We can never step outside our perceptual and cognitive systems to verify whether our experience corresponds to reality. We are, in a sense, trapped within our own minds, with direct access only to our representations, never to the things themselves.

While this might seem like cause for epistemological despair, Kant saw it differently. By recognizing these limitations, we can avoid the philosophical confusions that arise from assuming that our perceptions directly mirror external reality. We can still develop reliable knowledge within the framework of human experience, even if that knowledge is necessarily constrained by the structures of our minds.

Contemporary Neuroscience and the Constructed World

Modern neuroscience largely supports a constructivist view of perception that echoes Kant's insights. As neuroscientist Anil Seth puts it, "We don't just passively perceive the world; we actively generate it."[42] Our perceptions are best understood not as representations of an external world but as controlled hallucinations—predictions about the causes of sensory signals that are constrained, but not determined, by external reality.

This view helps explain many perceptual phenomena, from optical illusions to phantom limb sensations to psychedelic experiences. In all these cases, what we perceive is not directly mapped from sensory input but rather constructed by predictive processes in the brain that may or may not accurately reflect external conditions.

Recognizing this constructed nature of perception doesn't mean abandoning the concept of an external reality or the possibility of knowledge. Instead, it invites a more nuanced understanding of how perception works and a greater humility about the accuracy and completeness of our sensory experience.

Practical Implications of Perceptual Limitations

Our knowledge of the world is obtained through the senses, and therefore it is constantly subject to inaccuracy. The senses cannot provide access to absolute reality. Perceptions exist to help us translate what we perceive. They are there to guide us, not to show us the full truth; in fact, they hide the majority of it so we don't become overwhelmed.

This perspective has profound practical implications. If our sensory systems evolved primarily for survival and reproductive success rather than for delivering accurate representations of reality, then we should expect specific biases and limitations in our perceptions.[43] We should be particularly skeptical of perceptual intuitions in domains far removed from the environments in which our perceptual systems evolved.

For example, our intuitive physics works well for objects moving at speeds and scales relevant to everyday human experience but breaks down completely when applied to quantum or cosmic scales. Our social perception is exquisitely tuned to detect subtle signals in face-to-face interactions but may be misapplied when evaluating anonymous online communications or parasocial relationships with media figures.

Recognizing these limitations doesn't mean dismissing sensory experience as worthless. Rather, it means developing a more sophisticated relationship with our perceptions—trusting them in contexts where they're likely to be reliable while supplementing them with other forms of knowledge in contexts where they're likely to mislead.

PRACTICE: THE CHANGE BLINDNESS EXERCISE

Try this simple exercise to experience how your brain creates an illusion of complete visual awareness:

1. Find two nearly identical photographs online or create two versions of the same image where you've changed one significant detail (remove a person, change the color of a car, add or remove an object).
2. Look at the first image for exactly 10 seconds, taking in what you believe is the complete scene.

3. Immediately look at the second version with the change.
4. Notice how long it takes you to spot the difference—if you spot it at all.
5. Try this with a friend: show them the "before" image briefly, then the "after" image. Ask them to identify what changed.

This exercise demonstrates how your brain automatically compensates for sensory limitations by constructing a seamless perception of reality—even when that reality contains gaps.

Most people struggle to notice even dramatic alterations, such as entire people disappearing from scenes or major objects changing colors. This reveals a startling truth: despite feeling like we see everything in our visual field clearly and completely, we sample only small portions of our environment in detail.

This exercise demonstrates that your brain doesn't maintain a complete, detailed record of what you've seen. Instead, it creates a compelling illusion of comprehensive visual awareness while retaining only fragments and filling in the gaps with assumptions about what "should" be there.

Think about that for a moment. Your brain doesn't just translate reality—it actively edits, censors, and invents it.

OUR SENSES/THE SENSES

You walk through the world convinced you're seeing everything clearly, when in fact you're only capturing scattered details and unconsciously fabricating the rest.

And here's the truly mind-bending part: If your brain is willing to silently invent missing visual information and create false memories of scenes you've barely processed... what else might it be hiding from you? What other gaps might it be filling with fabrications so convincing you've never thought to question them?

> "The real voyage of discovery consists not in seeking new landscapes, but in having new eyes."
> —**Marcel Proust**[44]

As we conclude this chapter, consider how fundamentally your sensory experiences shape your understanding of reality. Your mind doesn't simply record the world around you; it actively constructs your experience through complex processes of filtration, interpretation, and prediction.

Your senses—vision, hearing, taste, smell, and touch—do not provide direct access to an objective reality. Instead, they offer a translated version shaped by the structure of your sensory organs, the architecture of your brain, your past experiences, your current emotional state, and your cultural conditioning. This translated reality is not a faithful representation of the world "as it is" but rather a pragmatic construction that has evolved to help you navigate your environment and meet your needs.

This understanding can be both humbling and liberating. Humbling because it reminds us of the fundamental limitations of human knowledge and the contingency of our perceptions. Liberating because it opens the possibility of experiencing the world differently by changing how we attend to sensory information and how we interpret what we perceive.

In the next chapter, we explore one of the most powerful systems of translation that shapes not just how we perceive the world but how we think about it—language. As you'll discover, the words we use don't just describe reality; they actively create it.

CHAPTER FIVE

LANGUAGE

"The limits of my language mean the limits of my world."
—**Ludwig Wittgenstein**[1]

Words are everywhere. They flow through our minds as thoughts, emerge from our mouths as speech, appear before our eyes as text. From the moment we wake until we fall asleep, we swim in an ocean of language. We use words to order coffee, express love, argue politics, tell stories, and even talk to ourselves when no one else is around.

But have you ever paused to consider what words actually are—those strange mouth-noises and squiggles on paper that somehow carry meaning from one mind to another? When I say "tree," how does that sound conjure in your mind the image of a tall, branching plant with leaves and bark? How do the arbitrary symbols that comprise an alphabet—which vary greatly across the world's 7,000+ languages—

manage to shape not just our communication but also our thoughts and perceptions of reality?

Language feels so natural, so transparent, that we rarely notice its profound influence on our consciousness. Yet, as we explore in this chapter, language doesn't just describe reality—it actively constructs it. The words available to us determine not only what we can easily express but also what we can readily think. Language is perhaps the most powerful and invisible filter through which your mind translates raw experience into meaning.

THE POWER OF LANGUAGE

Language is a tool unlike any other tool humans have created. A hammer extends our physical capabilities; language extends our cognitive capabilities. It allows us to share complex ideas, coordinate actions across time and space, accumulate knowledge across generations, and even think thoughts that would be impossible without words. As cognitive scientist Lera Boroditsky puts it, "Language is a uniquely human gift, central to our experience of being human."

How Language Shapes Reality

The idea that language influences thought—known as *linguistic relativity* or the *Sapir-Whorf hypothesis*—has sparked decades of debate among linguists, psychologists, and philosophers.² The strong version of this hypothesis, *linguistic determinism*, suggests that language entirely determines thought—that we cannot think thoughts for which we lack words. Most contemporary linguists and cognitive scientists reject this strong version. After all, we can coin new terms when needed, and people can think about and describe concepts even when their language lacks a single word for them. However, a more moderate version of the hypothesis—that language influences rather than determines thought—has found substantial empirical support.³

Examples Across Languages

Here's a fascinating example: Mandarin Chinese speakers think about time differently than English speakers. In Mandarin, speakers sometimes use vertical metaphors for time—describing earlier events as "up" (*shàng*) and later events as "down" (*xià*). Research shows that Mandarin speakers are faster than English speakers at arranging temporal sequences vertically and are more likely to think about time flowing from top to bottom, not just left to right.⁴ This doesn't determine what they think, but it likely affects how they mentally organize temporal relationships. And isn't it remarkable how the words available to us might shape not just how we communicate, but also how we perceive reality itself?

Numerous other examples demonstrate how languages carve up the world differently:

- The Pirahã people of the Amazon have no exact number words beyond "one," "two," and "many," and they have corresponding difficulties with exact counting tasks involving larger quantities.[5]
- Some languages, such as Kuuk Thaayorre (spoken in Australia), use absolute directions (north, south, east, west) instead of relative directions (left, right, front, back). Speakers of these languages maintain a remarkable sense of orientation at all times—they always know which way is north—and they organize their spatial thinking differently than speakers of languages that use relative directions.[7]
- German speakers, when describing events, tend to focus more on the endpoints and goals of actions than English speakers do, possibly because German grammar makes it easier to place verbs (and thus outcomes) at the end of sentences.

Words as Reality Filters

Many languages assign grammatical gender to nouns—meaning that objects like bridges, tables, or keys are classified as masculine, feminine, or neuter, even though they have no biological gender. Psychologist Lera Boroditsky conducted an experiment comparing how English and Spanish speakers describe a bridge. In Spanish, "bridge" (*puente*) is masculine, while in English it's simply neutral. Spanish speakers tended to use descriptive words like "strong" and "sturdy," while English speakers used more varied descriptions—suggesting that the grammatical gender assigned to a noun influences how speakers conceptualize that object.[8]

Consider how different your lived experience might be if your language lacked a word for "anxiety" but had twenty different words for subtle variations of what English speakers lump together as "contentment." Would you experience negative emotions, such as worry, differently? Would you be more attuned to positive emotional states? The vocabulary available to you doesn't just influence how you communicate about your experience—it also shapes the experience itself by directing your attention and providing cognitive categories.

Language as a Social Construct

Language is fundamentally a social construct—a system of symbols and rules created and agreed upon by communities to facilitate communication. Unlike the natural world, which exists independently of human perception, language relies on collective consensus to assign meanings to words and phrases. The meanings we attach to words are not inherent but rather shaped by cultural, historical, and social contexts.

The Arbitrary Nature of Signs

Swiss linguist Ferdinand de Saussure emphasized that the relationship between a word (the signifier) and what it represents (the signified) is arbitrary.[9] There's no inherent reason why the collection of sounds that make up the word "tree" should refer to a tall, woody plant. Different languages use entirely different sounds to refer to the same object, and nothing about the sounds themselves connects to the properties of the object.

This arbitrariness reveals language's constructed nature. The words we use aren't natural categories that reflect the world's true divisions; they're tools developed by human communities to serve practical purposes. The fact that we can translate between languages (however imperfectly) demonstrates that reality itself doesn't come pre-divided into the categories our particular language happens to use.

Language Communities and Shared Reality

Each language has its own unique set of rules and vocabulary that reflect the values and experiences of its speakers. For example, some languages have specific words for concepts that might require multiple words or phrases in another language. This discrepancy illustrates how language constructs our understanding of reality. By categorizing experiences and emotions into distinct words, we shape how we think about and interact with the world.

The anthropologist Franz Boas observed that detailed vocabularies develop in areas important to a culture.[10] Thus, languages spoken in Arctic regions have elaborate vocabulary for snow conditions. Languages in maritime cultures have detailed terms for tides and sea conditions, and languages in technological societies develop extensive terminology for their technologies.

These specialized vocabularies don't just facilitate communication about important topics; they also shape how community members perceive and categorize their experiences. Someone raised in a maritime culture doesn't just have more words for sea states—instead, they literally perceive more distinctions in what others might see as simply "rough water" or "calm water."

The Evolution of Language

Additionally, language is fluid and evolves over time. New words are created, meanings shift, and idioms develop as societies change. This malleability highlights that language is not a rigid framework but rather a dynamic tool that adapts to the needs and experiences of its speakers. However, this adaptability can lead to misunderstandings or ambiguities when individuals from different linguistic backgrounds attempt to communicate. This is why a lingua franca (a language that is adopted as a common language between speakers whose native languages are different) is so important.

Consider how the meaning of the word "literally" has evolved in recent years to sometimes mean its opposite—"figuratively." Or how the word "awful" once meant "inspiring awe" but now means "extremely bad." These semantic shifts don't happen according to any logical plan; they emerge organically through patterns of usage in communities.

Similarly, new technologies and cultural changes spark the creation of new terms. Words like "doomscrolling," "ghosting," and "FOMO (fear of missing out)," didn't exist a generation ago because the behaviors they describe weren't part of daily experience. As our collective reality changes, language evolves to help us navigate and make sense of that new reality.

THE BRAIN'S INTERPRETATION OF SOUND

The human brain processes language not only as a series of sounds but also as a complex interplay of meaning and context. However, this process is not infallible. Our brains can be easily tricked by auditory stimuli due to several factors, including the way we perceive sound, the context in which we hear it, and our cognitive biases.

From Sound Waves to Meaning

Language processing begins with sound waves hitting our eardrums but quickly becomes an intricate neural dance. When you hear someone speak, your brain doesn't simply register the sounds; it actively searches for patterns, attempting to match what you hear with stored templates of words and their meanings.

This pattern-matching process is remarkably flexible and resilient. You can understand someone speaking with an unfamiliar accent or in a noisy environment because your brain fills in missing information based on context and expectation, making language perception vulnerable to misunderstanding and manipulation.

One example of how our brains can be misled by sound is auditory illusions. Just as optical illusions trick our eyes into seeing something that isn't there, auditory illusions can cause us to hear sounds incorrectly. A well-known example is the "Yanny or Laurel" phenomenon, where listeners are divided over whether they hear the word "Yanny" or "Laurel." This difference in perception is influenced by factors such as the frequency of the sound and individual hearing abilities. The same auditory signal can be interpreted differently based on the listener's expectations, experiences, and even the acoustics of the environment.

The Phonemic Restoration Effect

Perhaps the most striking demonstration of the brain's active role in language perception is the *phonemic restoration effect*. If you hear a sentence where one phoneme (sound unit) is replaced by a cough or other noise, your brain will often "restore" the missing sound, making you perceive the word as complete.[11] Your brain doesn't just passively receive language; it actively constructs meaning, sometimes adding information that wasn't present in the original signal.

For example, if someone says "The *cough* is on the table" with the word "book" obscured by a cough, you'll likely hear "The book is on the table" without noticing anything unusual. Your brain fills in the missing information based on context and expectations. Remarkably, people often have high confidence in hearing the "restored" sound, believing they actually heard it rather than constructed it.

The Role of Context in Language Processing

Our brains rely heavily on contextual cues, such as body language, tone of voice, and situational factors, to interpret meaning accurately. For example, the same word can evoke different meanings depending on the situation or the tone in which it is delivered. For example, the word "fine" can convey approval in one context ("That's fine") and sarcasm in another ("Oh, that's just fine!").

The remarkable thing is that this contextual processing happens so quickly and automatically that we rarely notice it. In normal conversation, you don't consciously think, "I need to consider the context to understand what this person means." Your brain integrates linguistic input with contextual information seamlessly, creating the illusion that understanding language is a simple, straightforward process of hearing words and comprehending their meaning.

COGNITIVE BIASES IN LANGUAGE PROCESSING

When cues are absent or ambiguous, our brains may default to assumptions based on prior knowledge or stereotypes, and listeners may interpret a speaker's intent inaccurately. Moreover, the use of jargon, idiomatic expressions, or culturally specific references can further complicate understanding across linguistic and cultural boundaries.

Cognitive biases also affect how we interpret auditory information. For example, confirmation bias (discussed in Chapter 1) leads us to favor information that confirms our existing beliefs and dismiss information that contradicts them. In terms of language, confirmation bias can mean that we interpret spoken words in a way that aligns with our preconceived notions or expectations, potentially distorting our understanding of what is being communicated.

The Framing Effect in Language

How information is presented—the specific words chosen—can dramatically influence how we process and respond to it. Consider these two statements:

1. "The surgery has a 90% survival rate."
2. "The surgery has a 10% mortality rate."

These statements convey identical information, but research shows that people respond more positively to the first framing.[12] The negative connotations of "mortality" trigger different emotional and cognitive responses than the positive connotations of "survival," even though the statistical content is unchanged.

Politicians, advertisers, and media outlets are well aware of this framing effect and carefully choose their language to frame issues advantageously. "Tax relief" sounds different than "tax cuts," "climate change" evokes different responses than "global warming," and "enhanced interrogation" creates different mental images than "torture."

See Chapter 3 for a review of the framing effect.

The Availability Heuristic and Language

Additionally, the availability heuristic—a mental shortcut that relies on immediate examples that come to mind—can influence our perceptions. If a particular phrase or word is commonly used in our social circles, we may assume that it is universally understood, overlooking the possibility that it may not hold the same meaning for someone from a different linguistic or cultural background.

The availability heuristic (introduced in Chapter 1) explains why news coverage can distort our perception of reality. If news media heavily cover plane crashes but rarely mention car accidents, people may develop an exaggerated fear of air travel despite its being statistically much safer than driving. The language and stories available to us shape our understanding of what's common, important, or dangerous in the world.

The availability heuristic also influences our language behavior. We tend to use words and expressions that are easily available to us—terms we've heard recently or frequently. This result is feedback loops where certain ways of talking about topics become increasingly common within communities, further cementing particular linguistic frameworks for understanding the world.

LANGUAGE AND IDENTITY

Perhaps language's power is nowhere more evident than in how it shapes our sense of self. The words available to describe identities—whether related to gender, sexuality, occupation, nationality, or other aspects of selfhood—profoundly influence how we understand ourselves and others.

Linguistic Self-Construction

Psychologist Jerome Bruner argued that we create our sense of self through narrative—the stories we tell about who we are.[13] These narratives depend entirely on the linguistic resources available to us. If your language lacks words for certain ways of being or experiencing the world, then constructing an identity around those experiences becomes much more difficult.

Consider how the expansion of vocabulary around gender and sexuality has enabled many people to better understand and articulate their experiences. Terms like "non-binary," "demisexual," and "aromantic" don't create new ways of being human that didn't exist before. Instead, they provide linguistic tools that help people make sense of experiences they've always had but previously couldn't name in a single word.

Similarly, the presence or absence of certain identity labels in a culture's language significantly impacts how people in that culture conceptualize themselves. A person raised in a culture with a rich vocabulary for describing different types of intelligences might develop a more nuanced understanding of their own cognitive strengths and weaknesses than someone raised with a simpler linguistic framework that only distinguishes between "smart" and "not smart."

Code-Switching and Multiple Identities

Many multilingual people report feeling like slightly different people when speaking different languages.[14] A person might feel more formal and reserved when speaking Japanese, more expressive and emotional when speaking Italian, and somewhere in between when speaking English.

This phenomenon, sometimes called *language-dependent recall*, isn't just about cultural associations with languages. Different languages provide different tools for self-expression and self-understanding. The grammatical structures, vocabulary, and cultural concepts embedded in each language create distinct frameworks for experiencing and expressing one's identity.

Even within a single language, people often *code-switch*—altering their speech patterns, vocabulary, and tone depending on social context. The linguistic flexibility required to navigate different social spaces (professional, familial, friendly) reinforces the idea that our identities aren't fixed and singular. Instead, they are fluid and contextual, shaped by the linguistic tools we employ in different situations.

THE TOWER OF BABEL: LANGUAGE AND MISUNDERSTANDING

The biblical story of the Tower of Babel—where God confounds human language to prevent people from building a tower to heaven—contains a profound insight: Language differences create barriers to shared understanding and coordinated action. Although we've developed sophisticated translation tools, including Google Translate and ChatGPT, something is always lost when moving between languages.

The Challenge of Translation

Certain concepts resist precise translation because they're embedded in specific cultural and linguistic contexts. The German word *Waldeinsamkeit* describes the feeling of solitude and connectedness to nature when alone in the woods. The Arabic *tarab* refers to a state of musical ecstasy or emotional transformation that occurs when deeply moved by music or poetry. The Danish *hygge* evokes a quality of coziness and comfortable conviviality that creates a feeling of contentment.

These terms aren't just untranslatable because other languages lack equivalent single words; they're difficult to translate because they refer to culturally specific experiences that may not have exact parallels in other cultural contexts. They highlight how language doesn't just describe but also helps create distinctive ways of experiencing the world.

Even within a single language, perfect communication is rarely achieved. As psychologist Steven Pinker notes, when we speak, we're translating a web of thoughts into a linear string of words.[15] The listener must then reverse this process, using the words to reconstruct a web of meaning that ideally resembles the speaker's original thoughts. Given the complexity of this process, it's remarkable that we understand each other as well as we do.

Linguistic Misalignment and Conflict

Many interpersonal and social conflicts stem from linguistic misalignments—situations where the same words mean different things to different people, or where people lack shared vocabulary for discussing important concepts.

For example, in intimate relationships, words like "love," "commitment," or "respect" might carry subtly different connotations for each partner, creating situations where both people believe they're discussing the same thing but are actually talking past each other. In political discourse, terms like "freedom," "fairness," or "rights" function as powerful symbols that different groups define in fundamentally different ways.

Philosopher Ludwig Wittgenstein suggested that many philosophical problems arise from confusion about language rather than genuine metaphysical mysteries.[16] When we don't recognize that the same word can be used in different ways in different contexts, we may believe we're grappling with profound puzzles when we're actually just confused about meaning. Consider how we use the word "see." We say "I see the tree," "I see your point," and "I see what you mean." Philosophers might puzzle over what "seeing" really is, wondering if there's some deep connection between visual perception and understanding. But Wittgenstein would suggest we're just confused by language—these are simply different uses of the same word, not evidence of a profound metaphysical truth.

This insight applies well beyond philosophy. Many social and interpersonal conflicts that appear to be about substantive disagreements are actually linguistic confusions—situations where people are using the same

LANGUAGE

words to talk about different things, or different words to talk about the same things, without realizing it.

LANGUAGE AND THOUGHT: THE INNER VOICE

Most people experience what psychologists call "inner speech"—a kind of internal dialogue where we "talk" to ourselves using words, often in complete sentences. This inner voice isn't just a minor feature of our mental lives; for many people, it constitutes a significant portion of conscious experience and plays a crucial role in self-regulation, problem-solving, memory, and self-awareness.[17]

The Function of Inner Speech

Let's look more closely at the important cognitive functions of inner speech:

1. **Self-regulation**: By giving ourselves verbal instructions or encouragement, we can guide our behavior and maintain motivation. "Just one more set" or "Remember to breathe" are examples of inner speech that helps us regulate our actions.
2. **Problem-solving**: Talking through problems mentally allows us to apply linguistic logic to situations. When you mentally work through the steps of a difficult task, you're using inner speech to organize your thinking.

3. **Memory enhancement**: Verbally rehearsing (repeating) information helps us commit it to memory. When you repeat a phone number to yourself until you can write it down, you're using inner speech as a memory aid.
4. **Self-awareness**: Inner speech helps us reflect on our experiences and construct a narrative sense of self. The stories we tell ourselves about who we are and why we do what we do often take the form of inner dialogue.

The quality and quantity of inner speech varies widely among individuals. Some people report near-constant verbal thinking, while others experience thought more in terms of images, feelings, or abstract concepts. Some people's inner speech is abbreviated and telegraphic, while others report complete, grammatical sentences. These individual differences highlight the diverse ways language can structure thought.

Beyond Words: Non-Linguistic Thought

Inner speech plays an important role in cognition, but not all thinking is verbal. Research with pre-linguistic infants, non-human animals, and adults engaged in non-verbal tasks demonstrates that sophisticated thinking can occur without language.[18]

Some thoughts seem to happen too quickly for words. When an experienced musician improvises or an athlete makes split-second decisions, they're thinking without explicit verbal mediation. Similarly, the *tip of the tongue* phenomenon—knowing you know something but being unable to find the word—suggests that some knowledge exists in a form that precedes or transcends language.

Philosopher Eugene Gendlin developed a technique called *focusing* based on the observation that important insights often begin as vague, pre-verbal "felt senses" that only gradually can be articulated in words.[19] According to Gendlin, attending to these bodily felt meanings can help you access knowledge that isn't yet captured in language.

Non-linguistic forms of thought remind us that while language profoundly shapes cognition, it doesn't completely determine or contain it. There's always something that exceeds or precedes our verbal understanding—experiences that we struggle to put into words because they exist, at least initially, in nonverbal form.

METAPHOR: THE POET'S TRUTH

"Metaphors are much more tenacious than facts."
—Paul de Man[20]

At first glance, metaphors might seem like mere literary devices—ornamental language that makes speech and writing more engaging but doesn't fundamentally shape understanding. However, cognitive linguists such as George Lakoff and Mark Johnson have demonstrated that metaphor is not only a type of poetic language but also a fundamental mechanism through which we understand abstract concepts.[21]

Conceptual Metaphors in Everyday Thinking

We use metaphorical thinking constantly, often without realizing it. Consider these common expressions:

- "I can't grasp that concept."
- "Our relationship has hit a rough patch."
- "That rumor spread like wildfire."
- "She attacked my argument."
- "Time is flying by."

Each of these expressions reflects an underlying conceptual metaphor:

- UNDERSTANDING IS GRASPING
- RELATIONSHIPS ARE JOURNEYS
- IDEAS ARE LIVING THINGS
- ARGUMENT IS WAR
- TIME IS MOTION

These metaphors aren't just figures of speech. They are also conceptual frameworks that structure how we think about abstract domains. We don't just talk about arguments as if they were war; we actually experience them that way—developing strategies, defending positions, and winning or losing. The metaphors we use don't just reflect our thinking; they actively shape it.

Cultural Variation in Metaphorical Frameworks

Different cultures employ different metaphorical systems for understanding similar concepts. For instance, while English speakers tend to talk about time as if it were money ("spending time," "wasting time," "investing time"), this metaphor is less prominent in cultures with different relationships to commerce and temporal efficiency.

Similarly, while Western cultures often conceptualize the past as behind us and the future as ahead, some cultures, like the Aymara of South America, reverse this metaphor, conceptualizing the future as behind (because it can't be seen) and the past as ahead (because it can be known).[22]

These differences aren't just linguistic curiosities; they reflect and reinforce fundamentally different ways of experiencing time. A culture that metaphorically equates time with money is likely to produce different social practices, emotional experiences, and individual behaviors regarding time than a culture that uses different metaphorical frameworks.

The Power of New Metaphors

If metaphors structure our understanding of reality, then creating new metaphors can literally change how we experience the world. When Martin Luther King Jr. spoke of justice "rolling down like waters," and when environmentalists began describing Earth as a "mother" rather than a resource to be exploited, they weren't just creating vivid imagery; they were also proposing new conceptual frameworks that enable different ways of thinking about and relating to justice and nature.

In therapy, helping clients develop new metaphors for understanding their experiences can be transformative. Someone who conceptualizes depression as "being trapped in a dark hole" might experience their situation differently if they adopt a metaphor of depression as "a heavy fog that sometimes lifts." The new metaphor doesn't deny the reality of suffering but suggests the possibility of change in a way the "trap" metaphor doesn't.

This perspective gives new weight to poetry. Far from dealing merely in embellishment or entertainment, poets and other creative language users help forge the metaphorical frameworks through which we understand ourselves and our world. Their work isn't separate from "reality" but actively participates in constructing the realities we inhabit.

THE DEMOCRACY OF LANGUAGE: USAGE MAKES RIGHT

Unlike many human institutions, language has no central authority. While organizations like the Académie Française try to regulate language use, the reality is that language changes according to how people actually use it, not according to prescriptive rules. What begins as "incorrect" usage can become standard if enough people adopt it.

Descriptive versus Prescriptive Approaches

Linguists distinguish between descriptive approaches to language (which document how people actually use language) and prescriptive approaches (which establish rules about how people should use language).[23] While prescriptive rules have their place—especially in formal, institutional contexts—descriptive linguistics recognizes that language is fundamentally a living, evolving system that changes through use.

This democratic quality of language means that new words, meanings, and grammatical structures continuously emerge from the bottom up. Terms that begin as slang or jargon can enter the mainstream lexicon—"Google" transformed from a company name into a common verb meaning "to search online," while "selfie" evolved from informal slang to dictionary-standard vocabulary. Grammatical constructions once considered errors can become accepted standards as well. Using "they" as a singular pronoun was once deemed grammatically incorrect but has become widely accepted, and ending sentences with prepositions—once strictly forbidden by grammar teachers—is now perfectly natural in phrases such as "What are you thinking about?" Language doesn't follow top-down rules imposed by authorities; instead, it evolves organically through how people actually communicate, with yesterday's mistakes sometimes becoming tomorrow's proper usage.

Pronunciations too shift over time in response to social patterns rather than formal dictates.

Language Change and Power

Although language change happens organically through usage, not all speakers have equal influence over which changes become widely adopted. Historically, the language varieties spoken by socially powerful groups tend to become standardized, while varieties spoken by marginalized groups are often stigmatized as "improper" or "uneducated."

For example, England has historically deferred to royal speech patterns.

These dynamics reflect and reinforce social hierarchies. When a young person uses innovative language, they may be criticized for "not speaking properly." When a wealthy, educated person does the same, they might be praised for being "articulate" or "creative." These double standards reveal how judgments about language often serve as proxies for judgments about speakers' social value.

The critical sociolinguist James Paul Gee argues that what counts as "proper" language is always political.[24] The standard variety of any language attains its status not because it's inherently better or more logical than other varieties but because it's associated with socially dominant groups. Recognizing this truth can help us approach linguistic diversity with greater humility and curiosity instead of reflexive judgment.

The Beauty of Linguistic Diversity

Rather than seeing linguistic variation as a problem to be solved, we might better approach it as a resource to be appreciated. Different dialects, registers (levels of formality appropriate to different social situations), and styles of language offer different affordances—that is, different possibilities for expression and understanding.

African American Language, for instance, has grammatical features that allow for nuanced distinctions not easily expressed in Standard American English, such as the habitual "be" (as in "She be working" to indicate regular, ongoing action as opposed to current action).[25] Similarly, languages like Finnish with extensive case systems can express spatial relationships with a precision that requires more words in English.

Every language reflects the needs, values, and experiences of its speaking community. None is inherently superior to others, though each may be better suited to particular contexts or purposes. By approaching linguistic diversity with curiosity rather than judgment, we open ourselves to a richer understanding of the many ways human experience can be conceptualized and communicated.

LANGUAGE AS CONTROL: THE POLITICAL DIMENSION

"In a time of deceit, telling the truth is a revolutionary act."
—George Orwell[26]

Language isn't just a neutral tool for communication; it's also an instrument of social control. The words and conceptual frameworks available in a society's discourse shape what can be easily discussed, thought about, and questioned—and what remains difficult to articulate or challenge.

LANGUAGE

Orwell and Newspeak

In his dystopian novel *1984*, George Orwell imagined "Newspeak," a language designed by the totalitarian state to make certain thoughts literally unthinkable.[27] By eliminating words for concepts like freedom and democracy and replacing specific terms with vague, emotionally charged ones (such as "ungood" for "bad"), Newspeak aimed to restrict the range of thoughts possible within its linguistic framework.

While Orwell's vision was fictional, real totalitarian regimes have recognized and exploited language's power. Nazi Germany developed a specialized vocabulary that dehumanized victims and obscured atrocities. The Soviet Union created linguistic frameworks that made it difficult to articulate certain forms of dissent. In both cases, language wasn't just describing a changed reality; it was actively participating in creating and maintaining it. In Nazi Germany, bureaucratic, euphemistic language was used deliberately to mask brutality. Terms like *"Endlösung der Judenfrage"* ("Final Solution to the Jewish Question") were deployed to refer to the planned genocide of millions. The word *"Evakuierung"* ("evacuation") suggested relocation, but in practice referred to forced deportations to ghettos or death camps. Victims were often labeled *"Untermenschen"* ("subhumans") — a term applied to Jews, Slavs, Roma, and others — stripping them of personhood and justifying their extermination as a form of racial hygiene. Even in internal communications, phrases like *"Sonderbehandlung"* ("special treatment") were used as code for execution, allowing participants in the regime to talk about killing while psychologically distancing themselves from it.

Likewise, the Soviet Union developed a rigid ideological vocabulary that limited thought and suppressed dissent. Under Stalin, dissenters were labeled *"vrag naroda"* ("enemy of the people"), a term that justified arrests, torture, and executions with a veneer of moral clarity. The phrase *"counter-revolutionary agitation"* could be applied so broadly that any critique of the state became criminal. Words like *"kulak"* evolved from a term for a relatively prosperous farmer into a political slur used to justify mass dispossession, deportation, and execution. Entire categories of people were linguistically erased or dehumanized. During the Great Purge, the language of "confession" and "re-education" framed coerced false admissions as a kind of ideological cleansing. Soviet Newspeak, especially in later decades, stripped words of specific meanings—"democracy" and "freedom" were used in ways that bore little resemblance to their Western counterparts, making genuine critique nearly impossible.

In both regimes, language was not simply a reflection of power—it was a central tool of control. It shaped perception, normalized cruelty, and constructed a moral universe in which horrific acts could be justified, hidden, or even praised. Vocabulary did not merely describe a changed reality; it helped to manufacture it.

Doublespeak in Modern Discourse

Even in democratic societies, language is often deployed strategically to shape perception and control discourse. Linguist William Lutz identified several forms of doublespeak commonly used in political and corporate communication:[28]

1. **Euphemism**: Using mild, indirect, or vague terms for things that people might find distasteful or frightening (for example, "collateral damage" instead of "civilian casualties")
2. **Jargon**: Using specialized technical terminology to confuse or impress rather than to clarify (for example, complex financial terminology that obscures predatory lending practices)
3. **Gobbledygook**: Overwhelming the audience with a surplus of words (for example, dense, jargon-filled legal documents that hide important clauses in mountains of text)
4. **Inflated language**: Making the ordinary seem extraordinary through unnecessarily elaborate

language (for example, calling a used car "pre-owned luxury vehicle")

These linguistic strategies don't just describe reality differently; they construct different realities by making certain aspects of situations more salient while hiding others.

Reclaiming Linguistic Authority

Language can be used to control and manipulate, but it can also be used to resist control and create new possibilities. Throughout history, marginalized groups have often reclaimed slurs once used to demean them, transforming tools of linguistic oppression into powerful symbols of pride and solidarity. The LGBTQ+ community, for example, has embraced the word "queer"—once a cutting insult—as a broad, inclusive identity that challenges rigid norms around gender and sexuality. During the civil rights era, African Americans redefined the term "Black" as a positive marker of identity and cultural power, captured in affirmations such as "Black is beautiful" and the rallying cry of "Black Power." Feminist movements have reappropriated the words "bitch" and "slut" to confront sexist language and reclaim control over how women are labeled and judged, as seen in protests such as SlutWalk. Within disability activism, the term "crip"—formerly a derogatory shorthand for "cripple"—has been transformed into a marker of political identity and resistance. Even words like "nerd" and "geek," once used to mock, have been embraced by communities who now wear them as badges of intelligence, passion, and authenticity. These acts of linguistic reclamation show how language, far from being fixed, is a dynamic site of struggle—capable of both wounding and empowering, depending on who wields it and how. In addition, new vocabulary has been created to name experiences previously erased or ignored, from sexual harassment to microaggressions.

Feminist language reform has highlighted how seemingly neutral terms often embed gender bias and worked to create more inclusive alternatives.[29] Indigenous language revitalization movements fight to preserve not just linguistic heritage but also the unique ways of understanding and relating to the world encoded in those languages.

These efforts remind us that while language can function as a system of control, it can also be a site of resistance and creativity. By becoming more conscious of how language shapes our perception and by actively participating in creating new linguistic possibilities, we can expand the horizons of what can be thought, said, and ultimately experienced.

BREAKING FREE FROM LINGUISTIC CONSTRAINTS

If language shapes reality so profoundly, how can we ever see beyond the limitations of our particular linguistic frameworks? While we can never completely escape language's influence, several approaches offer ways to loosen its grip and expand our perceptual and conceptual horizons.

Mindfulness and Direct Experience

Mindfulness practices emphasize direct, non-conceptual awareness of experience. By attending to sensory experience without immediately labeling or categorizing it, we can temporarily suspend the automatic linguistic processing that usually mediates our relationship with reality.[30]

For example, when you look at a tree without immediately thinking "tree"—simply experiencing its colors, textures, movements, and relationships with its surroundings—you access a form of knowing that precedes and exceeds linguistic categorization. This direct perception doesn't negate conceptual understanding but complements it, providing a fuller, more immediate connection with experience.

Learning Multiple Languages

Learning additional languages provides concrete experience of how different linguistic frameworks structure reality differently. Bilingual or multilingual people often report that certain experiences or ideas seem more accessible or natural in one language than another.[31]

This linguistic flexibility creates a kind of meta-awareness— an understanding that any single linguistic framework is just one possible way of organizing experience. This awareness doesn't free us from language's influence but makes that influence more visible and therefore less determining.

Poetic and Artistic Expression

Writers and poets specialize in pushing language beyond its conventional limits, creating new combinations of words that expand what can be expressed and perceived. When Emily Dickinson writes of feeling "a funeral in my brain," or when James Baldwin describes love as "a battle, a war; love is growing up," they're not just creating vivid images but actually expanding the conceptual resources available within language.[32,33]

By engaging with poetry, literature, and other art forms that use language in unconventional ways, we can stretch our linguistic frameworks and develop greater flexibility in how we use language to understand our experiences.

Critical Awareness of Language

Perhaps the most powerful tool for breaking free from linguistic constraints is developing critical awareness of how language works. By studying linguistics, rhetoric, and discourse analysis, we can become more conscious of how language shapes our thinking and more intentional in how we use it.

This critical awareness doesn't mean rejecting all linguistic frameworks as equally arbitrary or adopting a position of cynical relativism. Rather, it means developing a more sophisticated relationship with language—one that recognizes both its profound power to shape experience and the possibility of using it more consciously and creatively.

PRACTICE: EXPANDING YOUR LINGUISTIC HORIZONS

Try these exercises to become more aware of how language shapes your perception and to expand your linguistic flexibility:

1. **Linguistic meditation**: Spend five minutes observing an ordinary object without naming it or describing it

mentally. Notice how the experience differs from your usual, language-mediated perception.

2. **Word collecting**: For one week, collect words from other languages that describe experiences or emotions that don't have simple equivalents in your language. Reflect on whether these concepts resonate with experiences you've had but couldn't easily name.
3. **Metaphor mapping**: Choose an important concept in your life (such as love, success, or health) and write down all the metaphors you commonly use to think about it. Then try to develop new metaphors that offer fresh perspectives on the same concept.
4. **Language detective**: Notice instances of politically charged language in news and social media. Identify how the specific words chosen frame issues in particular ways that encourage certain interpretations while discouraging others.

As you practice these exercises, you may begin to experience language not just as a tool for describing a pre-existing reality but as an active participant in creating the reality you experience. With this awareness comes greater freedom—not freedom from language's influence, but freedom to engage with language more consciously and creatively.

YOUR MIND: TRANSLATED

"Words do not just describe the world; they create the world they describe."
—John Searle[34]

As we conclude this chapter, consider how profoundly language shapes your experience of reality. The words available to you don't just describe your experiences; they actively structure those experiences, directing your attention to certain aspects of reality while leaving others difficult to notice or articulate.

This understanding can be both humbling and empowering. Humbling because it reveals that your most basic perceptions and thoughts are shaped by linguistic frameworks you didn't choose. Empowering because it suggests that by becoming more conscious of language's influence and more intentional in your use of it, you can expand the range of what you can think, perceive, and experience.

In the next chapter, we'll explore how this process of linguistic translation connects with another fundamental aspect of your experience—the complex relationship between your mind and your body. As you'll discover, the boundary between mental and physical experience is far more permeable than it might appear.

CHAPTER SIX

CONNECTION MIND/BODY

"There is more wisdom in your body than in your deepest philosophy."
—**Friedrich Nietzsche**[1]

Place your hand over your heart. Feel its steady rhythm beneath your palm. Now think about something that makes you anxious—perhaps an upcoming presentation or a difficult conversation you need to have. Notice what happens. Does your heartbeat quicken? Do your palms become slightly damp? Does your breathing change?

This simple exercise reveals something profound: Your thoughts directly influence your physical body. What happens in your mind doesn't stay in your mind—it cascades through your entire physical system, changing your heart rate, breathing, muscle tension, hormone levels, and countless other bodily processes.

Equally remarkable is the fact that this influence runs in both directions. Your physical state shapes your thoughts and emotions just as powerfully. When you slouch, your mood tends to darken. When you smile—even a forced smile—your emotional state shifts toward the positive. When you're sleep-deprived, your thinking becomes less creative and more pessimistic.

This chapter explores this intimate, bidirectional relationship between mind and body—how they communicate, influence each other, and ultimately form an integrated system that can't meaningfully be divided into separate "mental" and "physical" components. Understanding this connection offers profound insights into health, emotion, behavior, and the very nature of human experience.

THE MIND-BODY FACTORY

The undeniable bond between our minds and bodies plays a crucial role in our overall well-being. Think of the mind as a bustling factory, a hub of activity where feelings, thoughts, and emotions are processed and distributed throughout the body. This factory produces essential "goodies," like hormones and neurotransmitters, that help us feel energized, motivated, and healthy. Just like any factory, if things run smoothly, everything works harmoniously, but when disruptions occur the effects can ripple throughout our entire system.

The Biochemistry of Thought

What exactly happens in your body when you have a thought? While the complete answer remains one of neuroscience's greatest questions, we've discovered much about this remarkable process.

When you think, billions of neurons in your brain communicate through both electrical signals and chemical messengers called neurotransmitters.[2] Each thought activates distinct neural networks, creating patterns of activity that spread across your brain. These patterns don't stay contained in your head—they trigger cascades of signals that travel throughout your body via two main pathways: the nervous system and the endocrine (hormonal) system.

Your autonomic nervous system—the bodily system that controls involuntary functions such as heart rate and digestion—has two branches that respond to your thoughts. The sympathetic branch activates your "fight-or-flight" response, while the parasympathetic branch promotes "rest-and-digest" functions.[3] When you think anxious thoughts, your sympathetic nervous system increases your heart rate, dilates your pupils, and diverts blood from digestion to your muscles. When you think calming thoughts, your parasympathetic system does the opposite.

Meanwhile, thoughts also influence your hypothalamus, a brain structure that acts as a bridge between your nervous system and endocrine system. The hypothalamus signals your pituitary gland to release hormones that regulate everything from stress response (cortisol) to bonding (oxytocin) to pleasure (endorphins).[4] These hormones enter your bloodstream and affect virtually every cell in your body.

The Intelligence of the Body

Imagine waking up in the morning feeling energized and optimistic. Your mind is firing on all cylinders, releasing feel-good chemicals like serotonin and dopamine. Serotonin, often called the brain's natural mood stabilizer, plays a vital role in regulating emotions, promoting a sense of calm, and helping you feel grounded and steady throughout the day. It's also linked to sleep, digestion, and memory—key ingredients in overall well-being. Dopamine, in contrast, is all about motivation, anticipation, and reward. It fuels your drive to pursue goals, find pleasure in experiences, and feel a sense of accomplishment. When dopamine levels are healthy, even small tasks can feel satisfying and purposeful. Together, these two chemicals travel through your brain and body like a wave of sunshine—balancing your mood, sharpening your focus, and helping you meet the day with clarity and confidence. In this ideal scenario, the mind-body connection is in sync, and you feel capable, strong, and ready to take on challenges.

For these reasons, it's tempting to think of the brain as the command center that issues orders to a passive body. However, contemporary neuroscience reveals that intelligence is distributed throughout your body in remarkable ways. Your body isn't just receiving instructions from your brain—it's actively participating in cognition, emotion, and decision-making.

Consider your digestive system, which contains a network of 500 million neurons—often called the *second brain* or *enteric nervous system*.[5] This system doesn't just digest food; it also produces more than 30 neurotransmitters, including 95% of your body's serotonin. The state of your gut influences your emotions, and emotional stress directly affects gut function—a two-way communication system that explains why anxiety gives you "butterflies" and why chronic digestive issues often accompany mood disorders.

Your heart also demonstrates a form of intelligence. It has its own intrinsic nervous system of approximately 40,000 neurons that allow it to sense, regulate, and remember.[6] The heart communicates with the brain through neural, hormonal, and electromagnetic pathways. Research at the

HeartMath Institute has shown that heart rhythm patterns reflect emotional states, with positive emotions creating coherent patterns that improve cognitive function and negative emotions creating chaotic patterns that impair it.[7]

Even your immune system demonstrates cognitive-like capabilities. Immunologist Antonio Damasio describes immune cells as "thinking cells" that learn, remember, communicate, and make decisions about how to respond to different threats.[8] Your emotional state directly influences immune function, with chronic stress suppressing immune response and positive emotional states enhancing it.

The Embodied Mind

But what happens when stress levels soar? When life's pressures pile on, our "goodies factory" can begin to malfunction. Stress acts like a delivery truck that's overloaded or, even worse, misdirected. Instead of bringing in nourishing vitamins, it might deliver a surplus of cortisol, the stress hormone, which can leave you feeling anxious, fatigued, and overwhelmed. Your body starts to react to these unpleasant situations, signaling distress in various ways—tension in your shoulders, tightness in your chest, or fatigue that seems to settle in your bones.

The philosopher Maurice Merleau-Ponty argued that all consciousness is embodied: We don't just have bodies; we are bodies.[9] This perspective has gained scientific support through the field of embodied cognition, which examines how our physical bodies shape our cognitive processes.

Studies show that bodily states influence how we think in surprising ways:

- Holding a warm drink makes you more likely to judge others as having "warmer" personalities.[10]
- Leaning slightly forward leads to perceiving objects as closer than leaning backward does.[11]
- Making a fist increases men's self-perceived power.[12]
- Nodding your head while hearing an argument makes you more likely to agree with it.[13]

These effects aren't just metaphorical; they reflect how cognition is grounded in bodily experience. Abstract concepts like time, importance, and emotional states are understood through physical experiences such as movement, temperature, and position. When you describe a "heavy responsibility," "warm feelings," or "looking up to someone," you're using embodied metaphors that reflect how your body shapes your understanding.

This isn't just a coincidence; it's your body responding to the mental chaos you may be experiencing. If your mind is struggling under the weight of unrealistic expectations or negative thoughts, your body reflects that struggle. You might find yourself with headaches, digestive issues, or a general sense of malaise. These physical symptoms are your body's way of expressing what your mind has been suppressing, revealing the intricate connection that exists between them.

Interoception: The Inner Sense

Most of us are familiar with the five external senses—sight, hearing, touch, taste, and smell—but less familiar with *interoception*, the sense that allows you to feel your internal bodily states. Interoception lets you sense your heartbeat, breathing, hunger, fullness, and other internal conditions.[14]

Research shows that individuals vary significantly in interoceptive awareness, which is the ability to accurately sense these internal states. People with greater interoceptive awareness tend to experience emotions more intensely and make decisions more in tune with their physiological responses.[15] Conversely, poor interoceptive awareness is associated with anxiety, depression, and eating disorders.

Neuroscientist Antonio Damasio's *somatic marker hypothesis* suggests that emotions are fundamentally body-based signals that guide decision-making.[16] When you're faced with a decision, your brain draws on past experiences and simulates possible future outcomes. This simulation triggers subtle bodily changes—such as a tightening in your chest, a rush of warmth, or a slight unease in your stomach. These physical responses, known as *somatic markers*, act as internal signals or "gut feelings" that help steer you toward (or away from) certain choices. Importantly, these gut feelings aren't irrational or separate from logic. Instead, they work alongside reason, helping you weigh options more efficiently and avoid potential risks. In this way, the body doesn't just *react* to your decisions—it helps shape them, often before you're even consciously aware of it.

This perspective challenges the common view that emotions interfere with good decision-making. Instead, it suggests that your body's emotional wisdom complements analytical thinking. People with damage to brain regions that process bodily emotions often make poor decisions despite intact logical reasoning abilities—they can outline the pros and cons of different options but lack the somatic guidance to choose effectively.[17]

STRESS AND ITS PHYSICAL MANIFESTATIONS

Stress, in particular, can wreak havoc on the mind–body connection. When face overwhelming responsibilities—whether deadlines at work, family obligations, or financial worries—the body goes into a state of fight or flight. This natural response is meant to protect us, but in today's fast-paced world, it can become chronic. Our factory starts operating at full throttle, pumping out stress hormones continuously instead of the balanced blend of chemicals necessary for health and happiness.

The Evolution of Stress Response

The stress response evolved as a life-saving adaptation, preparing our ancestors to fight or flee from immediate physical threats such as predators. When we are facing danger, the *hypothalamic-pituitary-adrenal (HPA) axis* activates, triggering a cascade of hormonal changes that prepare the body for emergency action:[18]

- Adrenaline increases heart rate, elevates blood pressure, and boosts energy supplies.
- Cortisol increases glucose in the bloodstream and enhances the brain's use of glucose.
- Digestion, reproduction, and immune response are temporarily suppressed.
- Blood flow shifts from the brain's prefrontal cortex (responsible for rational thought) to limbic regions (responsible for emotional processing and survival behaviors).

These changes are well adapted for dealing with acute physical threats that require immediate action followed by recovery. The problem is that the same response activates when we face modern stressors such as traffic jams, looming project expectations, or relationship conflicts—situations where fighting or fleeing isn't helpful or possible.

Chronic Stress and Allostatic Load

Consider how you feel after a particularly stressful day. Your mind may be racing, filled with thoughts about what went wrong or what needs to be done tomorrow. As the mental noise amplifies, your body may start to tense up, your heart rate increases, and you might find it hard to relax. This reaction is not just a mental state; it's a physical manifestation of what's happening inside you. It serves as a reminder that you must pay attention to both your mental health and physical health.

Unlike our ancestors, who typically experienced stress in brief episodes with recovery periods, many modern humans live in chronically stressed states. When the stress response remains activated over the long term, it creates what scientists call *allostatic load*—the physiological wear and tear on the body from chronic overactivation of stress systems.[19]

This chronic stress manifests in measurable physical changes:

- Persistent elevated cortisol levels disrupt sleep, metabolism, and immune function.

- Blood vessels constrict, blood pressure rises, and inflammation increases.
- Muscle tension leads to pain, especially in the neck, shoulders, and back.
- Digestive processes slow, potentially causing irritable bowel syndrome and other gastrointestinal issues.
- Brain structure changes, with the amygdala (fear center) enlarging and the hippocampus (memory center) shrinking.

The link between chronic stress and disease is so well established that many researchers estimate that 60-90% of doctor visits are for stress-related conditions.[20] Heart disease, diabetes, depression, autoimmune disorders, and even cancer progression have been linked to chronic stress.

The Stress-Disease Pathway

Psychoneuroimmunology—the study of how psychological processes influence the nervous and immune systems—has revealed the biological pathways connecting mental stress to physical illness.[21] These pathways explain why, for example, students are more likely to catch colds during exam periods, or why caregivers for chronically ill family members show accelerated aging at the cellular level.

One key mechanism involves inflammation. Acute stress triggers inflammatory responses that help deal with injuries and infections. However, chronic stress leads to persistent low-grade inflammation throughout the body.[22] This chronic inflammation contributes to atherosclerosis (hardening of arteries), insulin resistance, neurodegenerative diseases, and many other health problems.

Another pathway involves telomeres—protective caps on the ends of chromosomes that preserve genetic information. Chronic stress accelerates telomere shortening, essentially speeding up cellular aging.[23] Studies show that people experiencing chronic stress—from caregiving to workplace pressures to discrimination—show telomere shortening equivalent to years of additional aging.

These findings demonstrate that the distinction between "mental health" and "physical health" is artificial. Stress isn't "all in your head"—it creates measurable, significant changes throughout your body that can ultimately lead to illness and premature death.

NATURE AS HEALER

One powerful remedy for restoring balance between mind and body lies in reconnecting with nature. Studies have shown that spending time outdoors can dramatically reduce stress levels, lower blood pressure, and improve overall mood. Nature acts as a soothing balm for our busy minds, providing a much-needed escape from the constant buzz of daily life. Whether it's taking a walk in the park, hiking through the woods, or simply sitting in a garden, these experiences can reset our internal factory, allowing it to shift back to a more productive and peaceful mode.

The Science of Nature's Benefits

The gentle sounds of rustling leaves, the fresh scent of grass, and the warmth of sunlight can all serve as reminders of what it feels like to be grounded and connected. When we immerse ourselves in natural settings, our minds often quiet down, and we become more attuned to our bodies. We begin to listen to what our bodies are telling us instead of pushing through discomfort or fatigue. This connection with nature helps us to find clarity, breathe more deeply, and feel a sense of belonging that can ease the burdens we carry in our minds.

The Japanese practice of *shinrin-yoku*, or "forest bathing," has sparked scientific research documenting nature's healing effects.[24] Studies show that spending time in forests:

- Reduces cortisol levels, blood pressure, and heart rate
- Increases parasympathetic nervous system activity (rest-and-digest response)
- Decreases sympathetic nervous system activity (fight-or-flight response)

- Strengthens immune function
- Improves sleep quality and duration
- Enhances mood and reduces symptoms of depression and anxiety

Even brief exposure to nature produces measurable benefits. Hospital patients with window views of natural settings recover faster and need less pain medication than those facing brick walls.[25] Office workers with plants in their workspace report 15% higher well-being and are 6% more productive than those in sterile environments.[26] Just 20 minutes in a park reduces stress hormone levels significantly, regardless of whether that time is spent exercising or sitting quietly.[27]

Biophilia: Our Innate Connection to Nature

Biologist E.O. Wilson proposed the *biophilia hypothesis*—the idea that humans possess an innate tendency to seek connections with nature and other forms of life.[28] This affinity isn't just cultural but biological, reflecting the environment in which humans evolved over millions of years.

Our sensory systems developed to process natural stimuli—the fractal patterns of tree branches, the gentle sound variations of flowing water, the earthy scents of soil and vegetation. Modern environments filled with straight lines, mechanical noises, and artificial smells lack the rich sensory information our nervous systems expect, potentially creating a form of sensory deprivation that contributes to stress and cognitive fatigue.

Attention restoration theory suggests that natural environments allow directed attention fatigue to recover.[29] Urban environments demand constant directed attention—to avoid traffic, navigate crowds, filter noise, and process information overload. Nature, with its "soft fascination," engages attention without demanding active concentration, allowing mental resources to replenish.

Bringing Nature into Healing

The mind-body benefits of nature have increasingly been incorporated into health care settings. Green prescriptions—physician recommendations to spend time in nature—have shown effectiveness comparable to medication for mild to moderate depression and anxiety.[30] Hospital gardens provide healing spaces for patients, visitors, and staff. Wilderness therapy programs help adolescents with behavioral issues develop self-regulation skills.

Even when physical access to nature is limited, research shows benefits from:

- Viewing nature photographs or videos

- Listening to nature sounds
- Having indoor plants
- Creating windows or skylights that frame natural views
- Using natural materials such as wood and stone in interior design

These approaches recognize that our bodies evolved in natural environments and respond positively to natural elements even in modern settings. By incorporating nature into our daily environments, we provide our minds and bodies with resources for self-regulation and healing.

YOUR BODY EXPRESSES WHAT YOUR MIND SUPPRESSES

Ultimately, it's essential to acknowledge that our bodies are not just vessels for our minds; they are integral to our overall experience of life. The phrase "Your body expresses what your mind suppresses" encapsulates this relationship beautifully. When we ignore our emotions—whether stress, anxiety, sadness, or even joy—our bodies may react in ways we cannot control. That reaction might be a sudden bout of illness, chronic pain, or even a feeling of fatigue that lingers long after the initial cause has faded.

Somatic Manifestations of Psychological Material

Our bodies often speak a silent language, conveying messages through physical sensations and symptoms. Think of it this way: When we suppress our emotions—whether consciously or unconsciously—we are like a shaken bottle of soda. The pressure builds, and eventually, it must find an outlet. This outlet might manifest as physical symptoms, such as headaches, muscle tension, digestive issues, or skin conditions.

For instance, when we feel anxious about an upcoming event, we might notice tightness in our chest or a knot in our stomach. These physical sensations are not just random occurrences. Instead, they are direct responses to our emotional state. They serve as reminders that we cannot compartmentalize our feelings without consequences.

Psychologist Alice Miller described how childhood emotions that couldn't be safely expressed get "stored" in the body, creating what she called "the body's never-forgetting memory."[31] These unprocessed emotions don't simply disappear; they remain as physical tension, altered posture, or disrupted physiological processes, potentially emerging later as physical symptoms.

Psychiatrist Bessel van der Kolk's research on trauma demonstrates how threatening experiences that overwhelm coping capacity become encoded in the body.[32] When trauma survivors are triggered, they experience not just psychological distress but also intense physical reactions—racing heart, shallow breathing, muscle tension—that reflect the body's unresolved traumatic memory.

The Language of Symptoms

Moreover, chronic pain can often be linked to unresolved emotional trauma or stress. Research has shown that fibromyalgia and chronic fatigue syndrome can have psychological components, with emotional distress exacerbating physical symptoms. This interplay between mind and body tells us that to achieve true wellness, we must address both our emotional health and physical health.

Medical anthropologist Gabor Maté proposes that many physical illnesses represent the body saying what the person cannot.[33] In his clinical work, he observed patterns connecting specific emotions to particular diseases:

- Autoimmune disorders often appear in people who chronically prioritize others' needs over their own.
- Digestive disorders frequently correlate with difficulty "digesting" life experiences or expressing anger.
- Respiratory conditions may develop in those struggling to "breathe" freely in their lives or relationships.

- Heart disease correlates with suppressed grief or unwillingness to acknowledge emotional needs.

While these connections aren't deterministic (many factors contribute to any illness), they highlight how specific emotions may manifest in corresponding physical systems. The body doesn't randomly generate symptoms but often expresses emotional material in symbolically appropriate ways.

The Wisdom of Physical Symptoms

From this perspective, physical symptoms aren't just problems to eliminate but potentially meaningful communications from parts of ourselves that haven't found other expression. Physician and author Lissa Rankin suggests approaching symptoms with curiosity: "What might my body be trying to tell me through this pain, fatigue, or illness?"[34]

This doesn't mean that all physical symptoms have psychological causes. Most illnesses involve complex interactions between genetic, environmental, lifestyle, and psychological factors. However, even with clearly physical conditions, psychological factors influence how symptoms develop, how severely they're experienced, and how effectively the body recovers.

Listening to our bodies is a crucial step in maintaining our overall well-being. By tuning into the signals our bodies send us, we can begin to unravel the emotional threads that contribute to physical discomfort. This practice requires mindfulness and self-awareness. For example, engaging in meditation, yoga, or journaling can help us reconnect with our feelings, providing an outlet for expression and reflection.

THE BODY AS EMOTIONAL ARCHIVE

Our emotional histories are stored not just in our memories but also in our physical bodies. The postures we adopt, the areas where we hold tension, even our breathing patterns reflect our emotional experiences and habitual responses to life situations.

Embodied Emotional Patterns

Body-oriented therapists have identified how emotional patterns become physically encoded:[35]

- Chronic anxiety often appears as shallow chest breathing and raised shoulders.
- Unexpressed anger frequently manifests as jaw tension and tight fists.
- Persistent sadness may show up as a collapsed chest and forward head posture.

- Shame often correlates with hunched posture and downcast eyes.
- Unresolved grief commonly appears as restricted breathing and chest constriction.

These patterns aren't just temporary reactions; with repetition, they become default physical states that persist even when the triggering emotions aren't consciously present. Eventually, these postures and tensions feel "normal" despite creating ongoing physical stress.

Alexander Lowen, founder of bioenergetic analysis, described this process as *muscular armor*—chronic muscle tension that originally developed to suppress unwanted emotions eventually becomes habitual.[36] This armor restricts not just physical movement but also emotional and energetic flow, creating both psychological rigidity and physical discomfort.

Body Memory and Trauma

Trauma researcher Peter Levine observed that traumatic experiences often leave physiological imprints that persist long after the events themselves.[37] When faced with overwhelming threat, animals in the wild naturally discharge stress energy through movement—running, fighting, or shaking. In contrast, humans often suppress these natural responses due to social constraints or prolonged threat situations, leaving the stress activation "locked" in the nervous system.

Imagine your brain is a big book. *Narrative memory* is how it remembers things by turning them into little stories—with beginnings, middles, and endings. Instead of just remembering facts or random images, you remember what happened, who was there, how you felt, and why it mattered—just like a story you'd tell someone. Brain scanning technologies now confirm that traumatic memories are stored differently than ordinary memories. Rather than being processed through the hippocampus into narrative memory, traumatic experiences often remain as fragmented sensory impressions in lower brain regions that control automatic physiological responses.[38] This explains why trauma survivors may experience intense physical reactions to triggers without clear mental memories of the original events.

Reclaiming Bodily Wisdom

When we allow ourselves to feel and acknowledge our emotions, we create space for healing. This doesn't mean that we will eliminate all stress or sadness from our lives; rather, it means we are developing a healthier relationship with our emotions. By recognizing that our feelings are valid and worthy of attention, we empower ourselves to take proactive steps toward increasing our well-being.

Somatic approaches to healing recognize that addressing the body is essential for resolving emotional issues. These practices include:

- Trauma-sensitive yoga, which helps a person reconnect with their body safely
- Somatic experiencing, which guides the completion of interrupted defensive responses
- The Feldenkrais Method, which uses gentle movement to re-educate the nervous system
- Dance/movement therapy, which uses expressive movement to process emotions
- Breathwork, which addresses restricted breathing patterns associated with emotional suppression

These techniques focus not on talking about emotions but on working directly with their physical manifestations. By changing bodily patterns, they create space for new emotional experiences and responses. Focusing on this connection reinforces the importance of a holistic approach to health. Integrating practices that nourish both the mind and body can lead to a more balanced, fulfilling life. In some cases therapy may be helpful in terms of teaching people how to process emotions, engage in physical exercise to release pent-up energy, and/or practice relaxation techniques to reduce stress levels.

THE EMERGING FIELD OF PSYCHONEUROIMMUNOLOGY

The scientific study of mind-body connections has flourished in recent decades, particularly in the field of psychoneuroimmunology (PNI)—the study of how psychological factors influence the nervous and immune systems.[39] This interdisciplinary field has transformed our understanding of how thoughts and emotions affect physical health.

The Communication Network

PNI research has revealed that the brain, nervous system, endocrine system, and immune system don't operate independently. Instead, they form an integrated network of constant communication. This network uses shared chemical messengers—neurotransmitters, hormones, and cytokines—that connect psychological experiences with physiological responses.[40]

What are cytokines? Think of your body as a big town where you live, and your immune system as the police officers and firefighters who keep everyone safe. When something bad happens—for example, when germs try to sneak into your town and make you sick—your body makes use of a special alarm system. This alarm system is composed of cytokines, which are like tiny messengers that run around shouting important messages to all the good guys in your body. When they spot trouble, they call out "Hey, we need more white blood cells to help us fight the bad germs!" or "Start fixing the hurt parts and make them better!" or "Quick, everyone work together to stop these nasty germs from spreading to other parts of our town!" Just as real alarms tell firefighters where to go and what to do, cytokines are the smart messengers that tell your immune system where the trouble is, what needs to happen to fix it, and when everything is safe again so they can stop working so hard.

In addition, immune cells have receptors for neurotransmitters and hormones produced during emotional states, allowing them to "sense" psychological conditions. Similarly, immune cells produce cytokines that cross the blood-brain barrier and influence brain function and mood. The *blood-brain barrier* is like a highly selective security system that protects your brain from potentially harmful substances circulating in your bloodstream. Think of your brain as a VIP area that requires special protection—the blood-brain barrier acts as an extremely careful bouncer, made up of tightly connected cells lining the blood vessels in your brain. This biological checkpoint blocks harmful substances such as toxins, bacteria, and most drugs from entering brain tissue, while still allowing oxygen and essential nutrients like glucose to pass through freely. The barrier maintains a stable environment for your brain by carefully controlling which chemicals can influence neural function. Certain cytokines can cross the blood-brain barrier, demonstrating the importance of communication between your immune system and brain. When immune cells produce cytokines that can breach the brain's protective filter, they gain the ability to directly influence brain function and mood—a process that highlights the intimate relationship between your physical health and your mental health.

The Mind-Gut Connection

One of the most active areas of mind-body research focuses on the gut-brain axis—the biochemical signaling between the digestive system and central nervous system.[41] The enteric nervous system in the gut contains more neurons than the spinal cord and produces more than 30 neurotransmitters, including 95% of the body's serotonin, a key mood regulator.

The gut also houses trillions of microorganisms collectively known as the microbiome, which influences both physical and mental health. Studies show that:

- Gut bacteria produce neurotransmitters that affect mood and behavior.
- Stress alters gut bacteria composition and gut barrier function. (The gut barrier is a protective lining in your

intestines that acts like a selective filter, controlling what can pass from your digestive system into your bloodstream.)
- Probiotics may reduce symptoms of anxiety and depression.
- Gastrointestinal disorders such as IBS (irritable bowel syndrome) show high comorbidity with anxiety and depression.

This research explains why we experience "gut feelings" and why digestive issues often accompany emotional distress. It also suggests new therapeutic approaches targeting the microbiome to address both psychological and physical conditions.

The Healing Response

Just as negative emotional states can contribute to illness, positive states can promote healing. PNI research shows that experiences of love, connection, meaning, and purpose produce measurable physiological effects that support health by:[42]

- Activating the parasympathetic nervous system, promoting relaxation and recovery
- Reducing inflammatory markers associated with chronic disease
- Enhancing immune function

- Promoting neurogenesis (growth of new brain cells)
- Increasing telomerase activity, which protects DNA and slows cellular aging

These findings help explain the placebo effect as a genuine healing response triggered by positive expectation, trust, and hope. They also elucidate why meditation, which cultivates positive emotional states, produces measurable health benefits ranging from reduced inflammation to improved cardiovascular function.[43]

Moreover, fostering connections with others can enhance our emotional health. Sharing experiences with friends or loved ones can lighten our emotional load, creating a sense of community and support. By engaging in meaningful conversations about our feelings and experiences, we not only lighten our burdens but also strengthen our connections with those around us.

EMBODIED PRACTICES FOR MIND-BODY INTEGRATION

Given the profound connections between mental and physical processes, practices that engage the body directly can be powerful tools for psychological well-being. Unlike approaches that focus primarily on verbal expression or cognitive understanding, embodied practices work with the direct experience of the body as a path to healing and integration.

Mindfulness-Based Approaches

Mindfulness practices involve bringing non-judgmental awareness to present-moment experiences, including bodily sensations, emotions, and thoughts.[44] Rather than analyzing or trying to change experiences, mindfulness involves observing them with curiosity and acceptance.

Jon Kabat-Zinn's Mindfulness-Based Stress Reduction (MBSR) program has demonstrated effectiveness in improving a wide range of conditions, including chronic pain, anxiety, depression, and immune function.[45] MBSR includes:

- Body scan meditation: systematically bringing attention to different body parts
- Mindful movement: gentle yoga with emphasis on present-moment awareness
- Sitting meditation: observing bodily sensations, emotions, and thoughts as they arise
- Informal practice: bringing mindful awareness to everyday activities

These practices help break the cycle of reacting automatically to stressors by creating space between stimulus and response. They also develop interoceptive awareness—the ability to sense internal bodily states—which research shows is key to emotional regulation.[46]

Movement-Based Approaches

While traditional exercise focuses primarily on physical fitness, many movement practices explicitly address the mind-body connection.

Yoga integrates physical postures, breathing techniques, and meditation to promote physical health and psychological well-being. Different styles emphasize various aspects of yoga, from vigorous physical practice (Ashtanga) to gentle therapeutic approaches (restorative yoga).[47]

Tai chi and **qigong** are Chinese movement arts that combine slow, deliberate movements with breath control and mental focus. Research shows that they reduce stress, improve balance and cardiovascular health, and enhance immune function.[48]

The Feldenkrais Method uses gentle, exploratory movements to increase body awareness and reorganize the nervous system. By breaking habitual movement patterns, it helps release chronic tensions and expand movement possibilities.[49]

5Rhythms and other conscious dance practices use movement as a form of moving meditation, allowing emotions to be expressed and processed through the body rather than through verbal analysis.[50]

These approaches recognize that psychological patterns manifest physically and that changing physical patterns can catalyze psychological shifts. By moving in new ways, we literally embody new possibilities for relating to ourselves and the world.

Breathing Practices

Breathing occupies a unique position in the mind-body relationship—it's both automatic and voluntary, both unconscious and conscious. It is a powerful bridge between physiological processes we can't directly control (such as heart rate or hormone secretion) and conscious awareness.[51]

Different emotional states create characteristic breathing patterns:

- Anxiety typically involves rapid, shallow chest breathing.
- Depression often features restricted, minimal breathing.
- Anger frequently appears as forceful, irregular breathing.

- Calm states are characterized by slow, deep, rhythmic breathing.

By deliberately changing breathing patterns, we can influence emotional states. For example, extending exhalation activates the parasympathetic nervous system, reducing stress and anxiety.[52] Breathing into areas of physical tension can help release emotional holding. Alternate nostril breathing (a yoga practice) can balance the autonomic nervous system and enhance cognitive function.[53]

These breathing practices are particularly valuable because they're accessible anywhere, require no special equipment, and produce immediate physiological effects that can interrupt stress cycles and create space for healthier responses.

THE BODY'S ROLE IN HEALING TRAUMA

Traumatic experiences pose particular challenges for mind-body integration. Whether from single overwhelming events (such as accidents or assaults) or chronic adverse experiences (such as childhood neglect or ongoing abuse), trauma can create profound disconnections between mind and body.

How Trauma Affects the Body

Trauma specialist Bessel van der Kolk describes trauma as fundamentally "a disorder of the physiology."[54] Brain imaging studies show that when trauma survivors recall traumatic memories or encounter triggers, brain areas involved in rational thinking become less active while areas controlling emergency responses become hyperactive. These responses suggest why trauma cannot be resolved through rational understanding alone.

Trauma can create two seemingly contradictory physical patterns:

- Hyperarousal: persistent activation of the sympathetic nervous system, creating chronic alertness, anxiety, and difficulties relaxing or sleeping
- Hypoarousal: shutdown responses including numbness, dissociation, and disconnection from bodily sensations

Oscillation between these extremes can create emotional and physiological instability

These patterns reflect survival adaptations to overwhelming circumstances—mobilizing to fight or flee when possible, shutting down to conserve resources when resistance seems futile. Although they are protective during traumatic events, these responses can become maladaptive when they persist long after danger has passed.

Body-Centered Approaches to Trauma Recovery

Recognizing trauma's physiological dimension, trauma specialists have developed approaches that specifically address its embodied aspects.

Somatic experiencing works to complete self-protective responses that were interrupted during traumatic events. By slowly and safely mobilizing defensive impulses (fight/flight) or completing immobility responses, it helps discharge trapped survival energy and restore nervous system regulation.[55]

Sensorimotor psychotherapy focuses on how trauma affects sensory processing, movement, and posture. It helps clients track bodily sensations and impulses, distinguishing present-moment experience from traumatic reactions and developing new physical resources for safety and agency.[56]

EMDR (Eye Movement Desensitization and Reprocessing) uses bilateral stimulation (typically eye movements, taps, or tones) while accessing traumatic memories. This approach appears to facilitate communication between brain regions, helping integrate fragmented traumatic memories into coherent narratives.[57]

Trauma-sensitive yoga provides opportunities to safely reconnect with the body through gentle movement practices specifically designed to respect trauma survivors' needs for choice, control, and predictability.[58]

These approaches share the understanding that trauma recovery requires not just changing thoughts or processing emotions but also restoring the body's capacity for self-regulation, safety, and pleasure. By working with the body directly, they address trauma's physiological imprints and help rebuild a sense of embodied safety and agency.

In summary, the connection between our minds and bodies is profound and intricately woven into our experiences of life. Our bodies serve as messengers, expressing what we may be suppressing in our minds. By acknowledging this relationship and learning to listen to our bodies, we can begin to address the underlying emotions that impact our physical health. Embracing a holistic approach to well-being allows us to cultivate resilience, enhance our emotional intelligence, and ultimately lead a more vibrant, fulfilling life. When we honor the wisdom of our bodies, we pave the way for a healthier, more integrated existence—one where both mind and body work in harmony.

CONNECTION MIND/BODY

PRACTICE: BODY SCAN MEDITATION

Take 10 minutes today to practice a simple body scan meditation:

1. Lie down or sit comfortably in a quiet space.
2. Close your eyes and focus on your breathing for a few moments.
3. Slowly direct your attention to different parts of your body, starting from your toes and moving up to your head.
4. For each area, notice any sensations without judgment—tension, relaxation, warmth, coolness, etc.
5. If you notice areas of tension, breathe into them gently.
6. Before finishing, take a moment to feel your entire body as a whole.

This practice can help you develop greater awareness of the physical manifestations of your mental and emotional states.

That knot in your stomach before an important meeting? The heaviness in your chest after an argument? The tension headache during a stressful day? These aren't just random physical discomforts—they're your body screaming what your mind refuses to whisper.

Your body keeps the score, faithfully recording truths your conscious mind would rather ignore. That persistent pain or mysterious illness might be telling a story your rational mind has worked overtime to forget.

> "The body says what words cannot."
> —Martha Graham[59]

As we conclude this chapter, consider how profoundly your mind and body communicate with and influence each other. Far from being separate entities, your mental and physical experiences form an integrated system with constant bidirectional communication. Thoughts and emotions cascade through your physiology, while bodily states shape your thinking and feeling.

This understanding dissolves the artificial divide between "mental" and "physical" health, revealing a more holistic perspective on human experience. Your anxiety isn't just "in your head," nor is your chronic pain merely "in your body." Instead, both involve complex interactions across your entire being.

By developing greater awareness of these mind-body connections, you gain access to multiple pathways for healing and growth. You can influence your emotional state through physical practices such as movement and breathing, just as you can affect your physical well-being through mental practices such as meditation and visualization.

In the next chapter, we explore how this integrated mind-body system interacts with other systems—specifically, how your translations of reality affect your relationships, and how others' translations affect you. As you'll discover, the connections within us lay the groundwork for the connections between us.

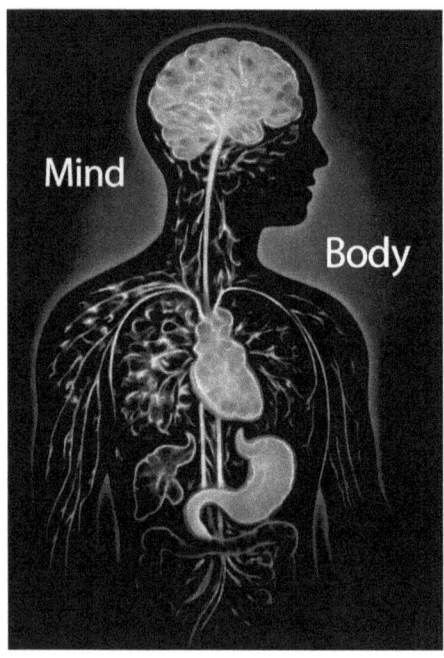

CHAPTER SEVEN

RELATIONSHIPS

"We don't see things as they are, we see them as we are."
—Anaïs Nin[1]

Close your eyes for a moment and picture someone you love deeply. What do you see? Perhaps you visualize their face, their expressions, the way they move or speak. You might feel warmth in your chest, a smile forming on your lips, a sense of connection and comfort. Now consider this provocative question: Is the person you're picturing the actual person who exists in the world, or is it your mind's translation of them?

The person you "know" is largely a creation of your own mind. The actual human being exists independently of your perception, but your experience of them—their meaning in your life, the emotions they evoke, your expectations of them—exists within your consciousness. The person you call "my partner" or "my friend" or "my parent" is actually a complex mental model built from your perceptions, memories, and interpretations.

This doesn't mean that your loved ones aren't real or that your connections aren't meaningful. But it does suggest something profound: Relationships don't just happen between two people. Instead, they happen between two sets of perceptions, two constructed realities that may overlap significantly or barely at all. Understanding how your mind creates your experience of others—and how their minds create their experience of you—can transform how you navigate the rich, complex territory of human connection.

THE SYMPHONY OF HUMAN CONNECTION

Imagine the human experience as an elaborate symphony, a grand orchestration of diverse instruments, each contributing its unique melody and rhythm to the collective sound. We are not a monolithic entity, but rather a vibrant mosaic of individuals, each a distinct note in the symphony of humanity. Our backgrounds, beliefs, and experiences shape our individual melodies, creating a rich and dynamic composition that is constantly evolving.

The Social Brain: Evolution's Masterpiece

Just as a symphony relies on the interplay of different instruments, human society thrives on the diversity of its members. Far from being a source of discord, our differences give our collective symphony its depth and complexity. It is through the harmonious blending of our individual voices that we create a truly remarkable and awe-inspiring masterpiece.

The human brain evolved specifically for social connection. Neuroscientist Matthew Lieberman argues that social connection is as fundamental a human need as food and shelter.[2] Our brains are wired to connect with others in ways that far exceed what's necessary for mere survival and reproduction.

Consider these remarkable adaptations:

- Newborn infants can recognize and prefer their mother's face within hours of birth, before they can focus their eyes properly on other objects.[3]
- Our brains contain specialized mirror neurons that activate both when we perform an action and when we see someone else perform the same action, creating a neural basis for empathy.[4]

- Our brains contain dedicated regions for facial recognition that can distinguish between thousands of different faces with remarkable accuracy.[5]
- Our bodies synchronize physiologically when we interact closely with others—our heart rates, breathing patterns, and even hormonal cycles align in what scientists call "coregulation."[6]

These adaptations aren't accidental. They reflect the fundamental importance of social connection for human survival and thriving. Throughout our evolutionary history, individuals who formed and maintained strong social bonds were more likely to survive and reproduce than those who didn't.

This evolutionary heritage means that connection isn't just a pleasant addition to life—it's a biological necessity. When we lack meaningful connection, our bodies respond as if they are facing a physical threat. Chronic loneliness increases stress hormones, impairs immune function, and raises the risk of numerous health problems from cardiovascular disease to dementia.[7] Conversely, strong social bonds promote physical health and psychological resilience, even extending life span.[8]

Underneath our social connections lies a complex interplay of biological drives and psychological defenses. Our understanding of "pleasure," for instance, is often clouded by societal judgments. Expressions of primal desires, such as those related to food or sex, are often stigmatized, while altruistic behaviors are lauded as virtuous. This dichotomy reveals a cultural bias that favors certain forms of pleasure over others, highlighting the influence of social norms on our perception of human behavior.

The Dance of Projection and Perception

Drawing a parallel from the animal kingdom, we can observe the behavioral dynamics of cichlid fish. When isolated, a male cichlid may exhibit aggression toward members of its own species, even turning against its mate. However, the introduction of an external rival, even if it is separated by a barrier, can redirect this aggression outward, resulting in a more harmonious relationship with the female cichlid. This example offers a compelling insight into human behavior. In close-knit social structures, such as marriages or military units, the inability to express aggression externally can lead to its displacement onto those closest to us.

This understanding empowers us to navigate our own emotional landscapes. Although we cannot always control the surge of primal emotions such as anger and irritation, we can cultivate the cognitive flexibility to transcend their immediate grip. By recognizing the transient nature of these emotions and resisting the urge to overidentify with them, we can mitigate their potential for harm.

Psychologist Carl Jung introduced the concept of *projection*—our tendency to unconsciously attribute our own unacknowledged thoughts, feelings, or traits to others.[9] We see in others what we cannot or will not see in ourselves, whether positive or negative. The qualities that most irritate us in others often reflect disowned aspects of ourselves. Similarly, the qualities we most admire may represent our own unrealized potential.

This phenomenon creates a fascinating paradox in relationships: Often, what we think we're reacting to in another person actually originates within us. The partner we experience as "controlling" may be activating our own repressed desire for control. The friend we see as "irresponsible" may embody freedoms we secretly wish for but deny ourselves.

These projections aren't random. They follow patterns established in our earliest relationships, particularly with caregivers. Attachment theory, pioneered by John Bowlby and expanded by Mary Ainsworth, explains how these early experiences create templates or "working models" for later relationships.[10] If our caregivers are consistently responsive, we develop secure attachment—a basic trust that others will be available when we need them. If care is inconsistent or inadequate, we may develop insecure attachment patterns characterized by anxiety, avoidance, or disorganization—chaotic, contradictory behaviors where we simultaneously seek and resist closeness.

These attachment patterns don't determine our relational destiny, but they do create powerful tendencies that influence how we perceive and interact with others. Someone with anxious attachment might interpret a partner's normal need for space as abandonment. Someone with avoidant attachment might experience a partner's bid for closeness as suffocating. In both cases, the perception says as much about the perceiver's internal working model as it does about the partner's actual behavior.

THE ALLURE OF THE FAMILIAR

Our brains are wired to seek familiarity, even when it's associated with pain. This innate preference for the known can lead us to cling to unhealthy relationships and patterns of behavior, and find solace in their predictability, even if they cause us suffering. This phenomenon, rooted in our survival instincts, highlights the powerful influence of the past on our present choices.

The Comfort of the Known

Why do we often recreate painful relationship patterns? Neuroscience offers some answers. From a neurobiological perspective, what's familiar is energetically efficient for the brain. Neural pathways that have been repeatedly activated—even those associated with pain—become well-established and require less energy to maintain than creating new pathways.[11]

This efficiency principle explains why we might unconsciously seek out relationships that feel familiar, even when that familiarity includes patterns of conflict, disappointment, or neglect that we consciously wish to avoid. If we grew up in a household where love was expressed through criticism or control, our brains might interpret these behaviors as signs of care, however dysfunctional. Conversely, healthier expressions of love might feel unfamiliar and therefore uncomfortable or even suspect.

The brain's bias toward familiarity creates a powerful form of emotional inertia. Breaking established patterns requires conscious effort, consistent repetition, and tolerance for the discomfort of novelty. It means recognizing when we're responding not to our current circumstances but to the echoes of our past.

The Compulsion to Repeat

Sigmund Freud observed that individuals who've experienced trauma often find themselves unconsciously repeating similar situations, a phenomenon he called *repetition compulsion*.[12] Rather than simply avoiding painful scenarios, we're drawn to recreate them, often with the unconscious hope of achieving a different outcome or mastering what once overwhelmed us.

This tendency appears throughout human relationships. The child of an emotionally unavailable parent may repeatedly choose partners who are similarly distant. The person who grew up amid unpredictability might be drawn to chaotic relationships that recreate that familiar landscape. In each case, there's an unconscious hope that this time, the story will end differently—that this time, they'll get the love, recognition, or safety that was missing before.

Breaking these cycles requires recognizing the pattern, understanding its origins, and consciously choosing different paths. It means tolerating the anxiety of the unfamiliar while building new neural pathways associated with healthier relationships. This process isn't quick or easy, but it offers the possibility of relationships based on current reality rather than historical patterns.

The Defense of Independence

A fierce insistence on independence often masks a deeper vulnerability. The belief that "I don't need anyone" can be a defense mechanism, a shield forged in the fires of past trauma. Perhaps an absent parent, an overworked caregiver, or a series of emotionally exploitative relationships have instilled a deep-seated distrust of others. These experiences teach us to rely solely on ourselves, fostering a sense of isolation that, while protective, can also be profoundly limiting.

This fortress of self-reliance guards against further heartbreak, but it can also become a prison, isolating us from the very connections we crave. It's a manifestation of the "fight" response, a survival mechanism designed to protect us from perceived threats. When this response becomes chronic, it can hinder our ability to form meaningful bonds and experience the full spectrum of human emotions.

Psychologist Robert Firestone describes what he calls the *fantasy bond*—a sense of connection that substitutes for real intimacy.[13] The fantasy bond preserves the illusion of a relationship while avoiding the vulnerability of genuine closeness. Those who have a fantasy bond with others go through the motions of relationship without emotional presence, maintaining connection through roles and routines rather than authentic engagement.

This protective strategy stems from early experiences where genuine vulnerability led to pain or disappointment. The child whose authentic expression was met with rejection or indifference may grow into an adult who substitutes performance for presence. The fantasy bond offers a compromise: the appearance of connection without the risks of true intimacy.

Breaking free from the fantasy bond requires recognizing when we're substituting form for substance in relationships—when we're physically present but emotionally absent, when we're playing a role rather than being ourselves. It means risking the vulnerability that the fantasy bond was designed to protect us from, and discovering whether that vulnerability might now lead to different, more fulfilling outcomes.

The good news is that trauma can be healed. By acknowledging the roots of our defensive patterns and challenging the limiting beliefs that perpetuate them, we can begin to dismantle the walls that separate us from others. This process requires courage, vulnerability, and a willingness to embrace the unknown, but the rewards—deeper connection, greater intimacy, and a more fulfilling life—are immeasurable.

FROM JUDGMENT TO UNDERSTANDING

Judgment is easy; understanding takes effort. It requires empathy, compassion, and a willingness to see beyond the surface. When we judge, we create division; when we understand, we foster connection. In its truest form, love is not a transaction or a possession; it's a state of being, a way of relating to ourselves and the world around us. True happiness lies not in external achievements or societal approval, but in aligning with our authentic selves, listening to the whispers of our hearts, and embracing the journey of becoming.

The Neural Basis of Judgment versus Understanding

Our brains are equipped with two distinct networks that enable different forms of social cognition. The *mentalizing network* helps us understand others' mental states—their thoughts, beliefs, intentions, and feelings.[14] The *mirror neuron system* allows us to directly experience others' emotions through a process of neural simulation.[15]

When we judge others, we're typically operating from the mentalizing network, making cognitive assessments based on assumptions, stereotypes, and past experiences. This network helps us categorize and make quick predictions about others' behavior, which can be useful for navigating social situations efficiently. However, it can also lead to oversimplification and error.

When we seek to understand others, we engage both the mentalizing network and the mirror neuron system. This combined activation allows us not only to think about others' perspectives but also to feel with them—to experience a form of neural resonance that creates the basis for empathy. This deeper engagement creates the possibility of genuine connection across differences.

Neuroimaging studies show that practicing compassion meditation activates both these networks while reducing activity in brain regions associated with judgment and self-reference.[16] These studies suggest that we can use deliberate practice to train ourselves to default to understanding rather than judgment.

The Cost of Constant Judgment

Judgment serves an evolutionary purpose. Our ancestors needed to quickly assess who could be trusted and who posed a threat. This capacity for rapid social evaluation helped ensure survival in environments where social belonging was essential and mistakes could be fatal.

However, in our complex modern world, this tendency toward quick judgment often creates more problems than it solves. When we reflexively judge others, we:

- Miss important contextual information that might explain their behavior
- Project our own biases, fears, and unresolved issues onto them
- Create unnecessary relationship conflict and distance
- Reinforce simplistic thinking rather than develop nuanced understanding
- Activate stress responses that affect both our well-being and our capacity for connection

Psychologists distinguish between evaluative judgment (good/bad, right/wrong assessments) and discernment (clear seeing without attached evaluation).[17] While discernment helps us navigate relationships wisely, evaluative judgment often creates barriers to authentic connection.

It's important to recognize that we rarely see others as they truly are; instead, we see them through the lens of our own experiences, biases, and unresolved issues. For this reason, two people can have completely different experiences with the same person. One might find the person warm and engaging, while another finds them cold and distant. The difference lies not in the person being observed, but in the observers themselves.

The Practice of Perspective-Taking

One way to improve our relationships is to approach them with greater curiosity and less certainty. Instead of assuming we know what someone else is thinking or feeling, we can ask them. Instead of reacting to our interpretation of their behavior, we can seek to understand their intention. This shift from projection to perception, from assumption to inquiry, can transform our relationships in profound ways.

Perspective-taking—the conscious effort to see situations from another's viewpoint—is a skill that can be developed with practice.[18] Research shows that regularly engaging in perspective-taking increases empathy, reduces prejudice, and improves relationship satisfaction.[19] It helps us recognize that others' behavior makes sense from within their reality, even when it seems irrational or problematic from our perspective.

Effective perspective-taking involves:

- Recognizing that your perception is just one possible interpretation, not objective reality
- Temporarily setting aside your emotional reactions to create space for curiosity

- Considering the factors that might be influencing the other person's behavior
- Imagining how the situation might look and feel from the other person's position
- Checking your understanding through respectful questions rather than assumptions

Perspective-taking doesn't require agreeing with others' perspectives or excusing harmful behavior. It simply means acknowledging the complexity of human experience and approaching differences with curiosity rather than judgment.

From Competition to Collaboration

Many relationship difficulties stem from approaching connection as a competition rather than a collaboration. When we see relationships as zero-sum games where one person wins and another loses, we create unnecessary conflict and miss opportunities for mutual benefit.

Game theory, a mathematical approach to strategic interaction, distinguishes between zero-sum games (where one player's gain is another's loss) and non-zero-sum games (where mutual benefit is possible).[20] Most human relationships are inherently non-zero-sum—both parties can gain through cooperation and communication.

When we approach relationships collaboratively, we:

- Look for solutions that meet both parties' core needs
- View differences as opportunities for greater understanding rather than conflicts to be won
- Remain curious about others' perspectives even when they differ from our own
- Recognize that supporting others' growth and well-being ultimately enhances our own

This collaborative mindset doesn't mean abandoning boundaries or always prioritizing others' needs over our own. Rather, it means recognizing that sustainable relationships require mutual benefit and seeking solutions that honor everyone involved.

THE INSIDE JOB OF HAPPINESS

Ultimately, happiness is an inside job. It's about cultivating self-acceptance, nurturing inner peace, and recognizing that our well-being does not depend on external circumstances or others' validation. It's about embracing the fullness of our human experience, with all its complexities and contradictions, and finding joy in the ongoing process of self-discovery.

The Relationship Paradox

When we look to others to fulfill us or complete us, we place an impossible burden on them. No one else can make us happy; they can only share in our happiness. Similarly, no one else can heal our wounds; they can only support us in our healing journey. The responsibility for our emotional well-being rests squarely on our own shoulders.

This need for self-reliance doesn't mean we don't need others. As social creatures, we thrive on connection and belonging. But these connections must be built on a foundation of self-love and self-respect. When we come to relationships from a place of wholeness rather than a lack thereof, we can give and receive love freely, without the desperate need for validation or approval.

Psychologist Carl Rogers observed the paradoxical aspect of human existence: "The more I am open to the realities in me and in the other person, the less do I find myself wishing to rush in to 'fix things.'"[21] When we accept ourselves as we are, we can more easily accept others as they are, without the compulsive need to change or control them.

This acceptance doesn't mean approving of all behaviors or staying in harmful situations. It means acknowledging reality as it is rather than as we wish it would be. From this clear-eyed perspective, we can make conscious choices about how to respond to what is, rather than react to what isn't.

Attachment Without Dependency

Healthy relationships involve attachment without dependency. We can be deeply connected to others while maintaining our sense of self and respecting their autonomy. This balance allows for intimacy without fusion, closeness without control.

Psychologist Murray Bowen described this capacity as *differentiation of self*—the ability to maintain a strong sense of self while remaining emotionally connected to others.[22] People with high differentiation can:

- Hold onto their thoughts and feelings even when others disagree
- Stay calm in the face of others' anxiety or criticism
- Maintain boundaries without building walls
- Experience deep intimacy without losing their sense of self
- Allow others their autonomy without feeling threatened or abandoned

Developing this capacity involves a dual process of strengthening our relationship with ourselves while learning to connect with others in ways that honor both parties' individuality. It means recognizing that true intimacy doesn't require sameness or agreement but rather the ability to remain connected across differences.

The Relationship as a Third Entity

Another helpful perspective focuses on seeing relationships as distinct entities that emerge from the interaction between individuals. Rather than person A and person B simply affecting each other, they co-create relationship C, which has its own characteristics and needs.

For this reason, nurturing a relationship becomes a shared creative project. Both parties contribute to creating a connection that serves the well-being of both individuals while developing qualities that neither person possesses alone. The relationship becomes a vessel for growth, healing, and discovery rather than simply a means of meeting individual needs.

This perspective shifts us from asking "What can I get from this relationship?" or even "What can I give to this person?" to "What can we create together?" It opens possibilities for connection that transcend the limitations of each individual while honoring their unique contributions.

By embracing our full humanity—our strengths and weaknesses, our light and shadow—we cultivate a deeper, more authentic connection with ourselves and others. We create space for joy, growth, and transformation. We become active participants in the grand symphony of life, contributing our unique melody to the collective composition, finding harmony in the beautiful diversity of human experience.

RELATIONSHIPS AS MIRRORS

> "In relationship, the process of revelation tells you what you are, your reactions, your prejudices, your whole background. In relationship there is a constant revelation, a constant discovery."
> —Jiddu Krishnamurti[23]

Our relationships serve as mirrors, reflecting aspects of ourselves that might otherwise remain invisible to our conscious awareness. Through our interactions with others, we encounter our fears, desires, judgments, and unresolved wounds. Each relational trigger offers an opportunity for self-discovery and growth.

Triggers as Information

When someone "triggers" us, they cause a disproportionate emotional reaction. These moments of heightened reactivity often point to unhealed wounds or unexamined beliefs within ourselves. Our partners, friends, and family members don't cause these reactions so much as activate pre-existing sensitivities.

For example, if a casual comment about your work performance sends you into a spiral of defensive anger, the intensity of your reaction may reflect earlier experiences where your competence was questioned or where failure led to rejection. The current situation has touched an old wound, creating a response that's more about historical pain than present reality.

These triggers aren't problems to be eliminated but rather signposts pointing toward areas that need attention and healing. When we recognize triggers as information rather than attacks, we can respond with curiosity rather than reactivity: "What is this strong reaction telling me about myself?" rather than "Why are they doing this to me?"

The Projection-Reflection Cycle

Much of what irritates or attracts us in others reflects disowned aspects of ourselves—the phenomenon that Jung called projection.[24] We project outward what we cannot or will not acknowledge inwardly. We engage in a continuous cycle of projection and reflection that shapes our relational experience.

This cycle operates in both positive and negative directions:

- We may project our unacknowledged talents onto others, seeing them as exceptionally gifted while downplaying our own abilities.
- We may project our disowned anger onto others, perceiving them as hostile while seeing ourselves as peaceful.
- We may project our repressed creativity onto others, admiring their expressiveness while ignoring our own creative impulses.
- We may project our denied vulnerability onto others, seeing them as needy while we maintain a façade of self-sufficiency.

In each case, our perceptions contain valuable information—not primarily about the other person, but about ourselves. The qualities that most capture our attention in others often reflect aspects of ourselves seeking recognition and integration.

Breaking this cycle requires developing self-awareness and taking responsibility for our projections. When we find ourselves reacting intensely to others—experiencing attraction, repulsion, or fascination—we can ask: "What might this reaction reveal about me? What part of myself am I seeing in this other person?"

The Gift of Difficult People

Some of our most challenging relationships offer the greatest opportunities for growth. The people who irritate, frustrate, or upset us most are often those who trigger our most sensitive wounds or challenge our most rigid self-concepts.

From this perspective, difficult relationships aren't obstacles to peace but rather potential catalysts for healing and expansion. The colleague whose communication style drives you crazy may be exposing your attachment to control. The family member whose life choices you judge harshly may be triggering your fear of disapproval. The friend whose neediness exhausts you may be reflecting your own unacknowledged needs for support.

Psychologist Robert Holden suggests asking a revealing question when facing relationship difficulties: "What is the gift in this situation that I'm not seeing?"[25] This question shifts us from victimhood to agency, from reactivity to receptivity. It opens the possibility that even painful relationships might be serving our personal growth in ways we haven't recognized.

None of this means accepting abuse or remaining in harmful situations. Some relationships require firm boundaries or even complete separation. But even these situations can offer important lessons about our values, needs, and capacity for self-care.

From Reaction to Response

When we recognize relationships as mirrors, we gain the freedom to respond consciously rather than react habitually. Instead of blaming others for our feelings or trying to change them to suit our preferences, we can use our reactions as opportunities for self-understanding and growth.

This shift from reaction to response involves several steps:

1. Pausing when triggered to create space between stimulus and response
2. Noticing our physical sensations, emotions, and thoughts but not reacting immediately
3. Recognizing when current reactions stem from past experiences
4. Taking responsibility for our own feelings without blaming others
5. Choosing a response aligned with our values rather than our conditioning

As we practice this process, we gradually develop greater emotional mastery and relational wisdom. We learn to use the mirror of relationship not to find fault but to find freedom from unconscious patterns that limit our capacity for authentic connection.

COMPASSION: THE HEART OF A RELATIONSHIP

At its core, the heart of a relationship is compassion—the ability to remain caring and open-hearted when we or others are struggling. Compassion differs from both empathy (feeling with others) and sympathy (feeling for others). It combines emotional resonance with the wish to alleviate suffering and the wisdom to respond skillfully.

The Science of Compassion

Research in neuroscience has identified distinct neural networks involved in different forms of empathy and compassion:[26]

- Emotional empathy activates brain regions involved in processing our own emotions, effectively creating a neural simulation of others' feelings.
- Cognitive empathy engages brain regions involved in perspective-taking and theory of mind. *Theory of mind* is the ability to understand that other people have their own thoughts, beliefs, and feelings that are different from your own. It's the mental skill that allows you to recognize that someone else might know something you don't know, or believe something that isn't true,

which is crucial for empathy, communication, and social interaction.
- Compassion activates brain regions associated with parental love, affiliative emotions, and reward.

While emotional empathy without compassion can lead to empathic distress and burnout, compassion appears to be nourishing and sustainable. It allows us to remain present with suffering without becoming overwhelmed by it.

Studies show that practicing compassion meditation not only increases prosocial behavior but also improves psychological well-being and reduces stress reactivity.[27] Unlike empathic distress, which activates threat responses, compassion activates the caregiving system associated with feelings of warmth, connection, and the motivation to help.

Self-Compassion: The Foundation

Contrary to common misconception, self-compassion isn't self-pity or self-indulgence. Psychologist Kristin Neff defines it as having three components:[28]

- **Self-kindness**: Treating ourselves with care and understanding rather than harsh judgment
- **Common humanity**: Recognizing that suffering and personal failure are part of the shared human experience

- **Mindfulness**: Holding painful thoughts and feelings in balanced awareness without over-identification

Research shows that self-compassion predicts psychological well-being better than self-esteem.[29] Unlike self-esteem, which often depends on comparison with others or external achievement, self-compassion offers a stable foundation for emotional health regardless of circumstances.

Self-compassion also serves as the foundation for compassion toward others. When we're harshly critical of ourselves, that critical energy tends to spill over into our relationships. Conversely, the more we practice kindness toward ourselves, the more naturally kind we become toward others.

Compassion in Action

In relationships, compassion manifests as the willingness to remain present with another's suffering without trying to fix, minimize, or avoid it. It involves honoring the other's experience while respecting their ability to find their own solutions.

Psychotherapist Carl Rogers defined *unconditional positive regard* as a fundamental acceptance of another person regardless of their behavior or feelings.[30] This doesn't mean approving of all of another person's actions, but rather maintaining a basic respect for the person's inherent worth and potential for growth.

Practicing compassion in relationships involves:

- Listening fully without preparing our response or trying to direct the conversation
- Validating others' emotions even when we don't share their perspective
- Responding to vulnerability with presence rather than advice or distraction
- Recognizing others' suffering without trying to immediately fix or change it
- Offering support in ways that empower rather than diminish

This compassionate presence creates a space where authentic connection can flourish. When we feel truly seen and accepted, we're more able to access our own wisdom and resources. Paradoxically, when we stop trying to change others, they become most open to change.

THE DANCE OF INTIMACY AND AUTONOMY

One of the fundamental tensions in relationships involves balancing connection with independence—that is, balancing the need for closeness with the need for freedom. Different people have different comfort levels with intimacy and autonomy, creating potential conflicts when these preferences don't align.

Attachment Styles and Relational Needs

Attachment theory provides a useful framework for understanding adult relationships. Research has identified four primary attachment styles:[31]

1. **Secure attachment:** Comfortable with both intimacy and independence; able to depend on others while maintaining autonomy
2. **Anxious attachment:** Strong desire for closeness; fear of abandonment; tendency to seek reassurance
3. **Avoidant attachment:** Emphasis on self-reliance; discomfort with deep intimacy; tendency to maintain emotional distance
4. **Disorganized attachment:** Conflicting impulses toward closeness and distance, often stemming from trauma

These attachment patterns develop based on early experiences with caregivers and significantly influence adult relationships. They affect everything from communication styles to conflict resolution to expressions of sexuality.

Understanding attachment patterns can help us recognize that different relational behaviors often reflect different needs and fears rather than different levels of caring. The partner who needs space isn't necessarily less committed; the partner who seeks closeness isn't necessarily too dependent. Both are responding to deeply ingrained patterns of relating that feel essential to their emotional safety.

The Pursuer-Distancer Dynamic

One common relationship pattern, identified by couples therapist Harriet Lerner, is the *pursuer-distancer dynamic*.[32] In this pattern, one partner seeks greater closeness (the pursuer) while the other seeks greater distance (the distancer). The more the pursuer pursues, the more the distancer distances, creating a self-reinforcing cycle that leaves both partners frustrated.

This dynamic often reflects complementary attachment styles—anxious and avoidant—creating a perfect storm of triggering interactions. The anxious partner's fear of abandonment triggers behaviors that activate the avoidant partner's fear of engulfment, whose resulting withdrawal then intensifies the anxious partner's abandonment fears.

Breaking this cycle requires both partners to move against their automatic tendencies. The pursuer practices giving space rather than chasing connection; the distancer practices moving toward rather than away from closeness. As each partner takes these counterintuitive steps, the relationship can find a new balance that honors both intimacy and autonomy.

Differentiation: The Key to Healthy Connection

Psychologist David Schnarch's concept of *differentiation* offers a path beyond the intimacy-autonomy dilemma.[33] Differentiation involves maintaining a clear sense of self while remaining closely connected with others. It allows us to be fully present in relationships without losing our identity or autonomy.

Highly differentiated individuals can:

- Hold onto themselves in the face of relationship pressure
- Tolerate discomfort that will result in growth
- Balance autonomy and connection
- Self-soothe rather than require others to regulate their emotions
- Stay present during conflict without shutting down or lashing out

Developing differentiation allows relationships to become containers for growth rather than simply sources of comfort or validation. It enables a form of intimacy that doesn't require fusion or the sacrifice of individuality. This path involves facing and working through our deepest insecurities and fears—what Schnarch calls "normal marital sadism." As we confront the ways we use relationships to avoid facing ourselves, we develop greater capacity for both self-regulation and deep connection. Paradoxically, the more complete we are within ourselves, the more fully we can join with others without losing ourselves.

COMMUNICATION: BEYOND WORDS AND TECHNIQUES

Effective communication is often cited as the cornerstone of healthy relationships. However, many conventional approaches to communication focus narrowly on verbal techniques while overlooking deeper aspects of communicative connection.

The Nonverbal Dimension

Research suggests that a significant portion of human communication occurs nonverbally, through facial expressions, body language, and tone of voice.[34] These nonverbal signals often communicate more reliably than words, especially regarding emotional states.

Our bodies constantly send and receive information below the threshold of conscious awareness. We react to others' micro-expressions, posture shifts, vocal tones, and pheromones (chemicals that humans unconsciously release and detect through smell, and which may influence attraction, mood, and social behavior) before our conscious minds register these signals. This nonverbal exchange creates what psychologist Daniel Stern called *attunement*—a synchronization of physical and emotional states between people.[35]

Attunement begins in infancy with the nonverbal dance between caregiver and child. Long before language develops, babies and caregivers communicate through gaze, touch, facial expression, and vocal tone. These early patterns form the foundation for later relational capabilities, including the ability to regulate emotions in connection with others.

In adult relationships, this nonverbal dimension remains crucial. When our words and nonverbal signals align, communication flows naturally. When they conflict—such as saying "I'm fine" through gritted teeth with crossed arms—the nonverbal message typically predominates, creating confusion and distrust.

Beyond Technique to Presence

Communication techniques can be helpful in a relationship, but their effectiveness can be undermined without the foundation of genuine presence. Techniques focus on what to say and how to say it, but presence involves who we are being in the interaction.

Presence includes the following qualities:

- Full attention without distraction
- Openness to the other's experience without judgment
- Emotional availability without defensiveness
- Authenticity without performance
- Curiosity without agenda

These qualities create a container of safety that allows for meaningful exchange beyond the specific words used. When we communicate from presence, even difficult conversations can strengthen connection rather than damage it.

Psychologist Carl Rogers observed that the most healing communication involves *congruence*—alignment between our inner experience and our outer expression.[36] This authenticity allows others to meet our true selves rather than our social performances, creating the possibility for genuine connection.

Listening as an Art Form

Most communication advice emphasizes speaking skills, but listening may be the more crucial and challenging skill. Genuine listening involves much more than waiting for our turn to talk or formulating our response while the other person speaks.

Deep listening includes:

- Suspending judgment and interpretation
- Attending to both content and emotional tone
- Noticing our own internal reactions without acting on them
- Being willing to be changed by what we hear
- Listening for the meaning beneath the words

Deep listening is both a gift to others and a practice of presence for ourselves. When we truly listen, we temporarily set aside our perspective to enter another person's world. This doesn't mean abandoning our own truth, but rather expanding our capacity to hold multiple perspectives simultaneously.

Poet David Whyte describes "the conversational nature of reality"—the understanding that truth emerges through genuine dialogue and does not reside exclusively in any single perspective.[37] This approach to communication moves beyond debate or persuasion toward co-creation of shared understanding.

TECHNOLOGY AND THE CHANGING LANDSCAPE OF CONNECTION

Our discussion of relationships would be incomplete without acknowledging how technology is transforming human connection. Digital communication, social media, and artificial intelligence are creating new possibilities and challenges for how we relate to each other.

The Digital Paradox

Digital technology has created unprecedented opportunities for connection across distances, cultures, and social boundaries. People find community, support, and even love online that might not be available in their immediate environment. Information flows freely, creating potential for greater understanding and collaboration.

At the same time, technology introduces new complexities into human connection. Research suggests several paradoxical effects:

- Social media use correlates with both increased social support and increased loneliness.[38]
- Digital communication facilitates connection across distance but may diminish the quality of in-person interactions.[39]
- Technology enables constant contact but may reduce deep presence and attention.[40]

- Online platforms offer unprecedented access to diverse perspectives but also create echo chambers that reinforce existing views.[41]

These mixed effects reflect not inherent properties of technology itself but rather how we use it. The same platforms that can strengthen relationships can also undermine them, depending on our intentions and behaviors.

Digital Literacy and Relational Intelligence

Skillfully navigating the digital landscape requires both technical knowledge and emotional awareness. This dual literacy helps us recognize how different technologies affect our neuropsychology, including our attention, memory, emotional processing, and social dynamics.

For example, research shows that:

- Notifications trigger dopamine release, potentially creating addictive cycles that fragment attention.[42]
- Text-based communication lacks emotional cues, increasing the likelihood of misinterpretation.[43]
- Scrolling social media activates social comparison, potentially increasing anxiety and depression.[44]
- Video calls require more cognitive processing than in-person conversations, creating "Zoom fatigue."[45]

Understanding these effects allows us to use technology more intentionally by choosing platforms and practices that enhance rather than diminish connection. We must recognize when digital communication serves relationships and when it substitutes for deeper engagement.

Creating Healthy Digital Boundaries

Healthy digital boundaries help preserve the quality of both online and offline relationships. These boundaries aren't about rejecting technology but rather using it mindfully and selectively.

Here are some helpful practices:

- Designating device-free times and spaces
- Using technology to arrange in-person connection rather than replace it
- Checking emotional motivations before posting or responding
- Engaging in regular digital detoxes to reset attention and presence
- Matching the communication medium to the message's emotional complexity

As with other aspects of relationships, the key lies in conscious choice rather than automatic habit. When we use technology intentionally, it can enhance our connections rather than depleting them.

PRACTICE: THE RELATIONSHIP MIRROR

Choose one challenging relationship in your life and ask yourself these questions: What aspects of this person trigger me the most? Could these triggers be reflecting something unresolved within myself? If I were to approach this relationship with curiosity instead of judgment, what might I discover?

Write down your reflections without censoring yourself. This exercise can help you recognize patterns in your relationships and identify opportunities for growth and deeper understanding.

Look around at the people in your life—those you love, those you hate, those who inspire you, and those who drive you crazy. What if I told you that none of them are who you think they are? That the version of them you interact with exists primarily in your mind?

The person you call your mother, your partner, your best friend, your enemy—each is a character created by your mind, viewed through the distorted lens of your needs, fears, and expectations. You're not relating to them; you're relating to your translation of them.

YOUR MIND: TRANSLATED

"The meeting of two personalities is like the contact of two chemical substances: If there is any reaction, both are transformed."

—Carl Jung[46]

As we conclude this chapter, consider how profoundly your perceptions shape your relationships. The people in your life aren't simply objective entities existing independently of your awareness; they are complex translations created by your mind based on actual interactions, filtered through your history, expectations, projections, and interpretations.

This understanding doesn't diminish the reality or importance of relationships. Rather, it invites a more conscious engagement with the inherently subjective nature of connection. By recognizing that your experience of others is partially your creation, you gain the freedom to examine and revise that creation.

Every relationship becomes an opportunity for self-knowledge and personal growth. The qualities that attract or repel you in others offer clues about your own inner landscape. The patterns that repeat across different relationships reveal your habitual ways of translating human connection. The triggers and reactions you experience provide doorways to healing unresolved aspects of yourself.

With this awareness comes the possibility of more authentic connection—connection based not on idealization or projection but on the humble recognition of both yourself and others as works in progress, each with its own complex interior worlds that can never be fully known but can be approached with curiosity, compassion, and presence.

In the next chapter, we explore the most fundamental questions raised by all these translations of reality: What is truth? If our minds so profoundly shape our experience of ourselves, others, and the world, is there such a thing as objective reality? And how might we approach the search for truth with both rigor and humility?

CHAPTER EIGHT

THE ABSOLUTE TRUTH

"There are no facts, only interpretations."
—Friedrich Nietzsche[1]

At the end of our journey through the mind's translations—how we perceive, think, feel, and relate—we arrive at perhaps the most profound question of all: What is true? If our senses, thoughts, emotions, and relationships are all shaped by our minds' interpretive processes, is there such a thing as objective reality? Can we ever know the absolute truth about ourselves, others, or the world?

These questions have haunted philosophers, scientists, and spiritual seekers throughout human history. Some traditions claim that absolute truth exists but lies beyond ordinary perception. Others suggest that truth is always relative to perspective, culture, or the practical needs that shaped human evolution—meaning that our understanding of reality may be filtered through mental frameworks that helped our ancestors survive rather than reveal objective truth. Still others propose that the very concept of "absolute truth" is itself a mental construction—another translation rather than a direct experience of reality.

In this final chapter, we explore these possibilities while considering what our journey through the mind's translations might mean for how we live. We won't arrive at definitive answers; that would contradict everything we've discovered about the nature of perception and understanding. Instead, we'll explore how awareness of our mind's translating tendencies might help us navigate life with greater wisdom, compassion, and purpose.

THE SPARK IN THE COSMOS

Consider for a moment the astonishing fact of your existence. You are made of atoms forged in the hearts of dying stars billions of years ago. These atoms have been recycled countless times through other stars, planets, and perhaps even other living beings, before temporarily coming together to form the body you currently inhabit. As astrophysicist Carl Sagan famously said, "We are a way for the cosmos to know itself."[2]

The Cosmic Perspective

From a cosmic perspective, human existence is exceedingly late in history. Our planet orbits an average star (the sun) in one of hundreds of billions of galaxies, each containing hundreds of billions of stars. The entire span of human civilization occupies less than a millisecond in the cosmic year. That is, if Earth's 4.5-billion-year history were compressed into a single calendar year, all of human history would fit within the final seconds of December 31st.[3]

This cosmic perspective doesn't diminish human experience but rather places it within a larger context. Our individual lives may be temporary arrangements of stardust, but that same stardust has allowed us to develop consciousness, language, art, science, and love—capacities through which the universe seems to have developed the ability to contemplate itself.

Physicist Brian Swimme suggests that the universe is not a collection of objects but rather a communion of subjects, and that consciousness in some form may be intrinsic to existence itself rather than merely an accidental byproduct.[4] In this view, human consciousness represents not an anomaly but rather a particularly complex manifestation of the universe's inherent capacity for awareness.

THE DANCE OF MATTER AND CONSCIOUSNESS

Throughout history, humans have debated the relationship between physical reality and consciousness. Are these separate domains (dualism), aspects of a single reality (monism), or something else entirely? While science has revealed much about the physical correlates of consciousness—that is, the neural processes associated with awareness—it has not resolved what philosopher David Chalmers calls the "hard problem" of consciousness: why and how physical processes give rise to subjective experience.[5]

What we can say with confidence is that consciousness and physical reality appear to be deeply intertwined. As quantum physics has demonstrated, the act of observation affects what is observed at the subatomic level. The famous "double-slit experiment" illustrates this conclusion perfectly: When scientists fire individual particles (such as electrons or photons) through two parallel slits toward a screen, the particles create an interference pattern as if they passed through both slits simultaneously—behaving like waves. However, when scientists place a detector to observe which slit each particle actually goes through, the wave-like interference pattern disappears and the particles behave like solid objects, going through one slit or the other. In other words, particles behave differently when they are observed than when they are not observed, suggesting an interdependence between consciousness and matter at the quantum level.⁶

While we should be cautious about drawing metaphysical conclusions from quantum mechanics, these findings do suggest that the relationship between mind and reality may be more complex than our everyday experience indicates. Reality may not be simply "out there" waiting to be perceived but may emerge through the interaction between awareness and potentiality.

Consciousness as Translation

Throughout this book, we've explored how consciousness translates raw sensory data into meaningful experience. This translation process isn't arbitrary—it evolved to help us survive and reproduce in specific environments. It's also not a direct representation of objective reality. Instead, it's a pragmatic construction, a usable model that allows us to navigate the world effectively.

Cognitive scientist Donald Hoffman proposes what he calls the *interface theory of perception*—the idea that our perceptions are more like a desktop computer interface than a faithful reproduction of reality.⁷ Just as desktop icons aren't literal representations of computer files but rather useful symbols that allow us to interact with those files, our perceptions may be simplified symbols that allow us to interact with reality rather than direct apprehensions of reality itself.

This perspective suggests that consciousness might be less a mirror reflecting reality than a translation system creating a workable interface with reality. The question then becomes not whether our translations are "true" in an absolute sense, but whether they're useful for the purposes that matter to us.

THE PRECIOUSNESS OF TIME

Our experience of time—its seeming abundance or scarcity, its swift passage or sluggish crawl—varies dramatically based on our mental state, activities, and stage of life. Time, like other aspects of experience, is profoundly shaped by our mind's translations.

The Perception of Time

Psychologists have identified numerous factors that influence our subjective experience of time:[8]

- Novel experiences seem to last longer than familiar ones.
- Time seems to pass more quickly as we age.
- Positive emotional states generally make time seem to pass more quickly.
- Pain and boredom make time seem to pass more slowly.

- Flow states (periods of complete absorption in an activity) can make time seem to disappear entirely.

These variations remind us that time, as we experience it, is not a uniform objective reality but rather a flexible subjective construct. As Einstein supposedly quipped when explaining relativity: "When you sit with a nice girl for two hours, it seems like two minutes; when you sit on a hot stove for two minutes, it seems like two hours. That's relativity."[9]

Mortality and Meaning

We often forget that our time is brief, behaving as if we'll live forever, postponing our happiness for some future date that may never arrive. We act as if we'll always have another chance to tell someone we love them, pursue our dreams, or experience wonder. Yet our time is limited, and this limitation makes our choices significant.

Psychologist Irvin Yalom argues that awareness of our mortality, while anxiety-provoking, can enhance our appreciation for life and clarify our values.[10] By acknowledging that our time is finite, we become more discerning about how we use it and more present for the experiences we choose to prioritize.

This awareness doesn't mean obsessing about death but rather allowing its reality to inform how we live. As the Stoic philosopher Seneca advised: "Let us prepare our minds as if we'd come to the very end of life. Let us postpone nothing. Let us balance life's books each day ... The one who puts the finishing touches on their life each day is never short of time."[11]

Chronos and *Kairos*: Two Types of Time

Ancient Greek distinguished between *chronos*—sequential, quantitative time measured by clocks and calendars—and *kairos*—opportune time, or the right or critical moment.[12] While modern society emphasizes *chronos*, focusing on efficiency and productivity, *kairos* invites us to attend to the quality and significance of moments rather than their duration.

Eastern philosophical traditions similarly distinguish between linear time and cyclical or eternal time. Zen Buddhism, for example, emphasizes living fully in each moment rather than being constantly oriented toward past or future. As Zen master Thich Nhat Hanh puts it: "The present moment is filled with joy and happiness. If you are attentive, you will see it."[13]

These alternative conceptions of time remind us that our conventional understanding of time as a scarce resource to be used efficiently is just one possible interpretation. By expanding our awareness to include different ways of experiencing time, we may discover greater richness and meaning in our temporal existence.

THE DECEPTION OF EMOTIONS

Emotions provide essential guidance for navigating life, but they can also profoundly distort our perception of reality. When we're anxious, the world appears threatening. When we're in love, it seems magical. When we're depressed, it looks bleak and hopeless. These emotional filters don't just add color to our experience; they fundamentally shape what we perceive, remember, and anticipate.

Emotional Intelligence and Meta-Awareness

Emotional intelligence involves not just experiencing emotions but also developing awareness of how emotions influence perception and behavior.[14] This meta-awareness — the ability to observe our emotional states rather than completely identifying with them — creates space between stimulus and response, allowing for more conscious choices.

Research suggests that this capacity for meta-awareness can be developed through mindfulness practices that cultivate non-judgmental attention to present experience.[15] By observing emotions as they arise and pass away, we can learn to recognize them as temporary mind states rather than absolute realities or aspects of our essential identity.

This doesn't mean suppressing or devaluing emotions. Rather, it means relating to them with greater wisdom and perspective. As psychologist Robert Augustus Masters notes, "Emotional maturity is not about not having emotions, but about being able to make room for all emotions and handle them in ways that don't harm ourselves and others."[16]

Cultural Variation in Emotional Experience

Our emotional lives are not purely biological. They are also shaped by culture, language, and social context. Different cultures recognize and emphasize different emotions, and even emotions that seem universal vary in how they're experienced and expressed across cultural contexts.[17]

For example:

- The Japanese concept of *ikigai* (one's reason for being or life purpose) has no direct English equivalent.
- The Japanese emotion of *amae* (dependence on another's benevolence) has no Western parallel.
- The Swahili term *polepole* means "slowly," conveying patience and a gentle pace of life, and conveying calmness and presence over haste.
- The Finish word *sisu* refers to a combination of determination, resilience, and inner strength in the face of adversity.

These cultural variations suggest that emotions, like other aspects of experience, are not fixed natural categories but rather constructions shaped by social learning and linguistic frameworks.[18] Different cultures develop emotional repertoires suited to their particular values, challenges, and social structures.

This perspective invites us to expand our emotional vocabulary and awareness, recognizing that our default emotional patterns reflect particular cultural translations rather than universal human responses. By learning from diverse emotional traditions, we may develop greater flexibility and nuance in how we experience and navigate feelings.

Emotions as Information, Not Commands

When we understand emotions as translations rather than direct perceptions of reality, we can relate to them as sources of information rather than commands to be obeyed.[19] For example, an emotion like anger provides information about perceived threats to our values or boundaries, but it doesn't dictate how we must respond to those threats.

This distinction is crucial for emotional wisdom. When we mistake emotions for reality itself—"I feel afraid, therefore the situation must be dangerous" or "I feel attracted to someone, therefore they must be right for me"—we surrender our capacity for discernment. When we recognize emotions as information-bearing signals within a broader context, we can incorporate their wisdom without being governed by our immediate impulses.

Psychologist Susan David describes *emotional agility* as the ability to face emotions with curiosity, compassion, and courage rather than seeking to control or avoid them.[20] This agility allows us to extract the valuable information that emotions provide while maintaining the freedom to choose responses aligned with our deeper values and long-term well-being.

THE TRIBAL MIND IN A GLOBAL WORLD

All human beings are born into tribes—groups with shared identity, values, and perspectives that shape how we understand ourselves and the world. These tribes may be based on family, religion, nationality, ethnicity, political affiliation, and/or countless other factors. Our tribal identities powerfully influence what we believe, whom we trust, and how we navigate moral questions.

The Evolution of Tribalism

Human tribalism has deep evolutionary roots. For most of our species' history, humans lived in small, close-knit groups of about 50 to 150 people. Survival depended on working together within the group and staying safe from outside threats. People who felt strong loyalty to their group and supported those closest to them—such as family, friends, and fellow group members—were more likely to survive and have children than those who didn't. [22]

This evolutionary heritage remains active in our psychology, creating an automatic tendency to:

- Trust members of our perceived in-group more than outsiders
- Adopt beliefs and values common within our group
- View our group's behaviors more charitably than similar behaviors in other groups
- Sacrifice individual interests for group welfare

These tendencies served adaptive functions in ancestral environments but can create significant problems in our complex, interconnected modern world. Historian Yuval Noah Harari notes in *Sapiens: A Brief History of Humankind* that while humans evolved to live in intimate communities, we now inhabit a world requiring cooperation among billions of strangers.[23] This mismatch between our tribal psychology and global challenges creates some of our most pressing social and political difficulties.

Morality: Universal or Tribal?

Our sense of morality—what we consider right and wrong, fair and unfair, virtuous and vicious—feels innate and universal. We typically experience moral judgments as perceptions of objective facts rather than subjective preferences or cultural conventions. "That's wrong" feels more like "That's poisonous" than "I don't like that."

However, anthropological and psychological research reveals enormous variation in moral systems across cultures and historical periods.[24] Practices considered morally obligatory in one culture (arranged marriages, physical punishment of children) may be considered morally repugnant in another. Even within cultures, moral perspectives vary significantly across political, religious, and social groups.

Psychologist Jonathan Haidt's *moral foundations theory* suggests that human morality builds on several innate foundations, including care/harm, fairness/cheating, loyalty/betrayal, authority/subversion, and sanctity/degradation.[25] However, cultures and individuals prioritize these foundations differently, creating distinct moral frameworks with their own internal logic and coherence.

This diversity doesn't mean morality is merely arbitrary or relative. As philosopher Joshua Greene argues, different moral systems may represent alternative solutions to the fundamental problem of enabling cooperative social life.[26] The variation emerges not because morality lacks purpose but because cooperation faces different challenges in different environmental and social contexts.

Understanding the tribal nature of morality doesn't require abandoning moral commitments. Rather, it invites a more humble, curious approach that recognizes the contingency of our moral intuitions while still engaging seriously with moral questions. As ethicist Susan Wolf suggests, we can combine "moral confidence with metaphysical doubt"—acting on our moral convictions while maintaining awareness of their limitations and openness to growth.[27]

Breaking Free from Tribal Thinking

Although tribal thinking comes naturally to humans, we're not doomed to remain confined within its limitations. Throughout history, individuals and movements have expanded the circle of moral concern beyond immediate group boundaries, recognizing the humanity and rights of those previously excluded.[28]

This expansion doesn't happen automatically. It requires deliberate effort to recognize and counteract our tribal biases. Some practices that can help include:

- Exposing ourselves to diverse perspectives, especially from those outside our primary identity groups
- Practicing perspective-taking—genuinely trying to understand how others see the world
- Examining the contingent factors (where and when we were born, our early experiences) that shaped our worldview
- Seeking common ground and shared values across group boundaries
- Distinguishing between criticizing ideas and dehumanizing people

These practices don't eliminate tribalism, but they do create space for more inclusive, nuanced thinking. They allow us to maintain connection with our primary identity groups while developing what philosopher Kwame Anthony Appiah calls *rooted cosmopolitanism*—an identity that honors particular roots while recognizing our place in a diverse human community.[29]

THE CAVE OF UNAWARENESS

The ancient Greek philosopher Plato offered a powerful metaphor for human perception and knowledge in his famous "Allegory of the Cave."[30] He described prisoners chained in a cave, able to see only shadows cast on the wall in front of them. These shadows, cast by puppeteers behind the prisoners, constitute the prisoners' entire reality. When one prisoner escapes and sees the actual world outside the cave, he returns to tell the others—who mock and reject his account, preferring the familiar shadows to the unsettling truth.

The Comfort of Illusion

Like Plato's cave dwellers, we often prefer the comfort of familiar illusions to the challenge of greater awareness. Our constructed realities—our habitual translations of experience—become comfortable homes that we're reluctant to abandon, even when they cause suffering or limit our potential.

This resistance to awareness operates both individually and collectively. Individually, we develop psychological defenses that protect us from threatening information about ourselves or the world. These defenses, such as denial, rationalization, and projection, maintain our self-image at the cost of self-knowledge.[31]

Collectively, societies develop what anthropologist Ernest Becker called *cultural hero systems*—shared frameworks of meaning that buffer existential anxiety by providing purpose and significance.[32] These systems offer comfort and direction but can also restrict vision and perpetuate harmful patterns when left unexamined.

The reluctance to expand awareness isn't simply stubbornness or ignorance. Challenging fundamental assumptions about self and reality creates genuine psychological discomfort, what psychologists call *cognitive dissonance*.[33] The deeper the potential insight, the greater the initial discomfort may be, which explains why transformative truths often meet significant resistance.

The Journey to Awareness

Despite these barriers, humans throughout history have pursued greater awareness—philosophical insight, scientific understanding, spiritual awakening, psychological integration. What motivates this counterintuitive journey from comfortable illusion toward uncomfortable truth?

Often, it begins with suffering. When our current translations of reality stop working effectively—when they repeatedly lead to pain, frustration, or a sense of meaninglessness—we become more willing to question our fundamental assumptions. As psychiatrist R.D. Laing observed, "There is a great deal of pain in life and perhaps the only pain that can be avoided is the pain that comes from trying to avoid pain."[34]

The journey continues through courage and curiosity—the willingness to face what is rather than what we wish were true, and the genuine interest in discovering what lies beyond our current understanding. It's sustained by communities and traditions that value truth-seeking and provide support for the sometimes disorienting process of expanding awareness.

The rewards of this journey aren't merely intellectual but also practical and experiential. Greater awareness typically brings:

- More effective navigation of reality, with fewer collisions with the actual nature of things
- Increased flexibility in responding to challenges, with more options beyond habitual reactions
- Deeper connection with others, as projections and assumptions diminish
- A sense of freedom and authenticity that comes from living in alignment with what is

Awareness Without Escape

Importantly, expanding awareness doesn't mean escaping human limitations or achieving some perfect, unmediated perception of absolute reality. We remain embodied beings with particular perspectives, operating through necessary translations of experience. The difference lies in our relationship to these translations—in recognizing them as useful constructions rather than confusing them with reality itself.

As philosopher Ken Wilber puts it, the goal isn't to avoid all maps but to avoid confusing the map with the territory.[35] When we recognize our perceptions, concepts, and beliefs as maps rather than territories, we can use them more skillfully while remaining open to their revision or replacement when they no longer serve us well.

This balanced approach avoids both naive realism (mistaking our translations for direct perception of reality) and nihilistic relativism (concluding that all translations are equally arbitrary and meaningless). It recognizes both the pragmatic value and the inherent limitations of our mind's translating processes.

EMBRACING FREEDOM AND PERSONAL TRUTH

If absolute, objective truth remains elusive—always filtered through our minds' translations---what remains as a foundation for living? This question haunted existentialist philosophers like Jean-Paul Sartre, who suggested that human beings are "condemned to freedom," or responsible for creating meaning in a world without inherent purpose.[36]

The Existential Challenge

The existentialist perspective sees both the terror and the opportunity in the human condition—our epistemic limitations combined with our unavoidable need to choose and act, which creates both the anxiety of radical responsibility and the potential for authentic self-creation. The terror lies in recognizing that we cannot escape responsibility for our choices by appealing to external authorities or absolute truths. The opportunity lies in the freedom to create authentic meaning through our commitments and actions.

Existentialism doesn't claim that everything is relative or arbitrary. Rather, it suggests that meaning emerges through the interaction between consciousness and world, through the ways we choose to engage with and respond to our circumstances. As Viktor Frankl, who survived Nazi concentration camps, wrote, "Between stimulus and response there is a space. In that space is our power to choose our response. In our response lies our growth and our freedom."[37]

The existential challenge is to live authentically in this space of freedom—to make conscious choices based on our deepest values rather than defaulting to social conventions, habitual reactions, or others' expectations. This authenticity requires both honest self-examination and courageous engagement with the world.

Personal Truth and Shared Reality

Although objective truth may elude us, we need not surrender to isolated subjectivity. We live in relationship with others and share a physical environment that imposes constraints on our possibilities. Our personal truths exist within this context of shared reality and mutual influence.

Philosopher Martin Buber described two primary ways of relating: I-It relationships, where we treat others as objects to be used or manipulated, and I-Thou relationships, where we engage with others as subjects with their own intrinsic value and integrity.[38] In I-Thou encounters, truth emerges not through imposing our perspective but through genuine dialogue that respects both self and other.

This dialogical approach to truth applies not only to human relationships but also to our engagement with the broader world. When we relate to nature, art, work, or spiritual questions with openness and respect for their otherness, we participate in co-creating meanings that transcend purely personal preference while avoiding claims to absolute authority.

INTEGRATION: THE PATH OF WISDOM

Wisdom traditions across cultures suggest that truth lies not in extremes but in integration—that is, in finding the middle way between opposing perspectives. Rather than choosing between absolute objectivity and pure subjectivity, between determinism and unlimited freedom, between social convention and radical individuality, wisdom seeks the partial truths within each polarity.

This integrative approach doesn't resolve all contradictions into tidy solutions. Rather, it develops the capacity to hold paradox—to recognize the truth in seemingly contradictory perspectives without forcing premature resolution. As physicist Niels Bohr noted regarding quantum mechanics, "The opposite of a correct statement is a false statement. But the opposite of a profound truth may well be another profound truth."[39]

Integration also applies to the relationship between rational thinking and other ways of knowing. While critical reasoning provides essential tools for evaluating claims and detecting errors, it has limitations. Intuition, embodied knowing, emotional intelligence, aesthetic sensitivity, and relational wisdom offer complementary approaches that may access truths unavailable to reason alone.

By honoring multiple ways of knowing while maintaining critical awareness, we develop a more comprehensive, textured understanding than any single approach can provide. This integration doesn't guarantee perfect knowledge, but it does offer the most complete translation currently available to us as complex beings in a complex world.

The Paradox of Being Human

Throughout this book, we've explored how our minds translate reality—filtering, interpreting, and constructing our experience rather than simply recording objective facts. We've seen how these translations affect our sensory perceptions, thoughts, emotions, and relationships, creating the unique subjective worlds we each inhabit.

This exploration reveals a fundamental paradox of human existence: We are simultaneously the translators of our experience and the translated. We create our reality through our perceptual and cognitive processes, yet we ourselves are created by forces beyond our control—evolutionary history, cultural context, family dynamics, random events, and countless other factors that shape who we become.

The Limited Author

We are not the sole authors of our lives. We didn't choose our genes, our early environments, the historical era or culture we were born into, or many of the formative experiences that molded our personalities and perspectives. The very brain that translates our experience was itself shaped by factors outside our choice or control.

Yet neither are we merely passive products of these influences. Within constraints, we possess agency—the capacity to reflect on our experience, question our assumptions, make choices, and participate in shaping our development. This agency isn't absolute freedom but rather what philosopher Daniel Dennett calls *evolvability*, or the ability to respond adaptively to circumstances and gradually expand our possibilities.[40]

The paradox of being simultaneously shaped and shaping creates both humility and empowerment. Humility comes from recognizing the countless influences that created our current perspective; empowerment comes from realizing that this perspective remains open to evolution through our conscious participation.

The Cosmic Perspective Revisited

Returning to the cosmic perspective with which we began this chapter, we might ask: What does it mean to be temporary arrangements of stardust capable of contemplating our own existence? What significance can we find in lives that are vanishingly brief against the backdrop of cosmic time?

Astronomer Carl Sagan suggested that our cosmic insignificance and our cosmic significance are two sides of the same coin: "We are like butterflies who flutter for a day and think it is forever." Yet these ephemeral butterflies have developed mathematics, art, ethics, and science—capacities that allow us to comprehend aspects of reality far beyond our immediate experience.[41]

Our lives may be brief, but they participate in an ongoing process of cosmic evolution. The atoms that temporarily constitute "you" have existed since shortly after the Big Bang and will continue to exist in new forms long after your death. The insights, creations, and connections you generate may influence others in ways that extend far beyond your individual lifespan.

This perspective doesn't eliminate death anxiety or solve the human search for meaning. Instead, it offers a context in which transience and significance can coexist—where being "dust" doesn't preclude having purpose. As physicist Brian Swimme puts it, "You take hydrogen gas, and you leave it alone, and it turns into rosebushes, giraffes, and humans."[42]

Our existence may be temporary, but it's also astonishing.

CREATING MEANING IN A MEANINGLESS UNIVERSE

If the universe itself doesn't provide inherent meaning or purpose, as many contemporary philosophers and scientists suggest, then meaning becomes something we create rather than discover. This viewpoint doesn't claim that life is meaningless but rather that meaning emerges through our engagement with life rather than existing independently of human consciousness.

The Absurd and Its Transcendence

Philosopher Albert Camus described the human condition as "absurd"—a contradiction between our desire for meaning and the universe's silence.[43] We long for clear purpose, moral certainty, and cosmic significance, yet find ourselves in a world that offers no guarantees of these things.

Camus rejected both despair and false comfort. Instead, he advocated "facing the absurd"—acknowledging the absence of inherent meaning without surrendering to nihilism. For Camus, meaning emerges through how we choose to live in relationship with the absurd: through rebellion against meaninglessness, through passionate engagement with life, and through solidarity with others facing the same fundamental condition.

This perspective doesn't offer the security of absolute meaning, but it does provide the dignity of creating meaning through conscious choice. Rather than receiving purpose from external authority, we assume responsibility for defining and pursuing what matters most to us.

The Creation of Value

Existentialist philosophers argue that values are not discovered but rather created through our choices and commitments.[44] When we act as if something matters—justice, beauty, knowledge, love, or countless other possibilities—we bring that value into existence through our dedication to it.

This doesn't mean that values are merely subjective preferences or arbitrary decisions. Instead, they emerge through our interaction with the world and with others, reflecting both our individual consciousness and our embeddedness in nature and culture. The values we create are genuine responses to real aspects of our situation, even without claims to absolute authority.

The creation of value happens not primarily through intellectual assertion but through lived commitment. Values become real when embodied in action—when we organize our lives around what matters to us and accept the consequences of those choices. As philosopher Jean-Paul Sartre noted, "Man is nothing else but what he makes of himself."[45]

Sources of Meaning

While each person must ultimately determine what gives their life meaning, certain sources of meaning appear consistently across cultures and throughout history. These include:

> **Connection**: Deep bonds with others, with nature, or with something perceived as sacred or transcendent
>
> **Contribution**: Making a positive difference in the lives of others or in the broader world
>
> **Comprehension**: Understanding ourselves and reality more clearly and completely
>
> **Creativity**: Bringing something new into existence through art, innovation, or personal development
>
> **Challenge**: Engaging with difficulties that stretch our capabilities and promote growth

Research in positive psychology suggests that lives incorporating multiple sources of meaning tend to be more fulfilling than those focused exclusively on a single source.[46] This diversity provides resilience when particular sources of meaning become temporarily unavailable and honors the complexity of human needs and capacities.

The specific forms of these sources vary widely. One person might find meaning through raising children, another through scientific research, another through artistic creation, another through spiritual practice. The particular expression matters less than the authentic alignment between our deepest values and how we actually live.

A FINAL REFLECTION: DUST WITH PURPOSE

We are, indeed, dust—temporary configurations of matter and energy that will eventually disperse and reconfigure into other forms. Yet even dust has a purpose within the unfolding story of the cosmos. Stellar dust forms planets, soil dust nurtures plants, and the dust that constitutes human beings has somehow developed the capacity to contemplate its own existence and wonder about its meaning.

The Gift of Awareness

The journey we've taken through this book—exploring how our minds translate reality—represents a uniquely human gift: the capacity to become aware of our own perceptual and cognitive processes. Unlike other species that simply perceive according to their biological programming, we can recognize our translations as translations, opening possibilities for greater flexibility, creativity, and wisdom in how we relate to ourselves and the world.

This meta-awareness doesn't free us from the necessity of translation. We remain embodied creatures with particular perspectives, operating through interpretive frameworks shaped by evolution, culture, and individual history. But awareness of these processes allows us to hold our translations more lightly—to use them without being completely used by them, to modify them when they no longer serve us well, and to consider alternatives that might offer fresh insights.

Living Without Ultimate Answers

I have no definitive advice to offer about how you should live. Self-help books, religious authorities, political ideologies, and philosophical systems all offer useful perspectives, but they remain limited by the inherent constraints of human understanding.

Rather than providing answers, this book has invited questions—questions about how you perceive, think, feel, and relate; questions about what you take for granted and what you might reconsider; questions about how you create meaning in a world without guaranteed purpose.

These questions have no definitive answers. They represent ongoing inquiries that evolve as we evolve, shifting with our circumstances and understanding. Their value lies not in reaching conclusive resolution but in promoting the continuous expansion of awareness that characterizes the most fulfilled human lives.

Finding Your Way

While I offer no universal prescription for living, this exploration of the mind's translations suggests certain attitudes that might serve you well on your unique journey:

> **Curiosity** about your own perceptual and cognitive processes, about perspectives different from your own, and about the mysteries that remain beyond current understanding
>
> **Compassion** toward yourself and others as you navigate the challenges of existence with limited vision and inevitable mistakes
>
> **Courage** to question familiar assumptions, face uncomfortable truths, and create meaning through conscious choice rather than passive acceptance

Creativity in developing translations of reality that serve your deepest values while remaining open to revision as a result of your experiences

Connection with others through authentic engagement that respects both commonality and difference in how we translate our shared world

These attitudes don't eliminate the fundamental uncertainties of human existence. Instead, they offer resources for living meaningfully within those uncertainties—for creating purpose even in a universe that doesn't guarantee it, for finding significance even in our temporary arrangement of cosmic dust.

PRACTICE: VALUES CLARIFICATION

Take time to identify your core values—the principles that truly matter to you, not those imposed by society or others' expectations. Write down 5 to 7 values that resonate deeply with you (such as authenticity, compassion, growth, and/or freedom). For each value, reflect on:

1. How this value shows up in your life currently
2. One small step you could take to align more closely with this value in the coming week

This exercise will help you move beyond abstract concepts toward living your personal truth more fully each day.

THE ABSOLUTE TRUTH

Remember that the meaning you create through how you live isn't diminished by its personal nature or its ephemeral nature. A sand castle washed away by the tide isn't worthless because it doesn't last forever. Its value lies in the creativity of its creation, the joy of its brief existence, and perhaps the memories it leaves with those who encountered it.

Your life—your particular translation of cosmic dust into conscious experience—matters precisely because you decide it matters, because you invest it with purpose through how you choose to live. In a universe without guaranteed meaning, the meaning you create becomes all the more precious for being freely chosen rather than externally imposed.

> "We are going to die, and that makes us the lucky ones. Most people are never going to die because they are never going to be born.... We privileged few, who won the lottery of birth against all odds, how dare we whine at our inevitable return to that prior state from which the vast majority have never stirred?"
> **—Richard Dawkins** [47]

As our journey through the mind's translations concludes, we return to where we began—to the astonishing fact of our existence and the remarkable capacity for awareness that allows us to contemplate it. We've explored how our minds filter, interpret, and construct our experience rather than simply recording objective reality. We've examined how these translations shape our perceptions, thoughts, emotions, and relationships, creating the subjective worlds we each inhabit.

This exploration hasn't led us to absolute truth or definitive answers. It has instead invited a more conscious relationship with our own meaning-making processes—a recognition of both the necessity and the limitations of our translations. It has suggested that wisdom lies not in escaping translation but rather in translating more consciously, more flexibly, and with greater awareness of the inherent partiality of all human understanding.

The path forward isn't toward perfect perception but toward more skillful engagement with reality as we encounter it, neither clinging to our current translations as absolute truth nor dismissing all translations as equally arbitrary. It's a path of continuous learning, growth, and refinement, guided by the values we choose to embody and the meanings we create through how we live.

In this light, the mind's translations aren't obstacles to overcome but capacities to develop—tools that can become increasingly subtle, versatile, and aligned with our deepest purposes. By bringing awareness to how we translate reality, we open possibilities for translating in ways that

THE ABSOLUTE TRUTH

reduce suffering, enhance understanding, deepen connection, and increase freedom for ourselves and for those whose lives we touch.

May this awareness serve you well on your continued journey.

A NOTE FROM THE AUTHOR

Thank you for joining me on this exploration of the mind and its many translations of reality. My hope is that this book has offered you not just insights into how your mind works, but also practical tools to help you navigate life with greater awareness, compassion, and authenticity.

Remember that understanding the mind's fallibility isn't about diminishing its wonder—it's about freeing yourself from the tyranny of unexamined thoughts and perceptions. When we recognize that our minds are translating reality rather than directly experiencing it, we open ourselves to greater possibilities and deeper connections.

The practices included throughout these chapters aren't just theoretical exercises. They're invitations to experience reality differently, to question your automatic interpretations, and to cultivate a more conscious relationship with your thoughts, emotions, and sensory experiences.

May this book be a starting point on your journey toward greater self-awareness. The real learning happens not in reading these words, but in living them—in bringing

A NOTE FROM AUTHOR

mindful attention to the countless moments when your mind is busily translating your experience.

With deep appreciation for your curiosity and openness,

Jack Hernandez

ACKNOWLEDGMENTS

This book exists because of the countless conversations, chance encounters, and shared moments that have shaped my understanding of the human mind. To every person whose story, question, or perspective sparked my curiosity about how we think, feel, and make sense of our inner worlds—thank you. Each interaction, whether brief or lasting, contributed something vital to these pages.

I am deeply grateful to every individual I have crossed paths with throughout my life. The teacher who challenged my assumptions, the stranger on the train who shared an unexpected insight, the colleague who asked the question I couldn't answer, the friend who listened patiently as I worked through complex ideas—you all played a role in bringing this work to life. Our shared humanity is woven throughout every chapter.

To my partner, whose unwavering support sustained me through the long hours, the moments of doubt, and the joy of discovery that marked this writing journey—your belief in this project never wavered, even when mine did. Your patience, encouragement, and understanding made it possible for me to explore these ideas fully and fearlessly. This book is as much yours as it is mine.

ACKNOWLEDGMENTS

Finally, to anyone who will read these words and find something meaningful within them, thank you for allowing me to be part of your own journey of understanding. The mind, in all its complexity and wonder, connects us all.

Notes

Chapter One: Identifying Yourself with Thoughts

[1]Tolle, E. (2004). *The Power of Now: A Guide to Spiritual Enlightenment*. New World Library.

[2]Gazzaniga, M. S. (2011). *Who's in Charge? Free Will and the Science of the Brain*. Ecco.

[3]Jung, C. G. (1969). *The Archetypes and the Collective Unconscious*. Princeton University Press.

[4]Nin, A. (1961). *Seduction of the Minotaur*. Swallow Press.

[5]Marshall, J., & Arikawa, K. (2014). Unconventional colour vision. *Current Biology*, 24(24), R1150–R1154.

[6]Zimmermann, M. (1989). The nervous system in the context of information theory. In R. F. Schmidt & G. Thews (Eds.), *Human Physiology* (pp. 166-173). Springer-Verlag.

[7]Eagleman, D. (2011). *Incognito: The Secret Lives of the Brain*. Pantheon.

[8]Libet, B., Gleason, C. A., Wright, E. W., & Pearl, D. K. (1983). Time of conscious intention to act in relation to onset of

cerebral activity (readiness-potential). The unconscious initiation of a freely voluntary act. *Brain*, 106(3), 623–642.

[9]Kurzban, R. (2010). *Why Everyone (Else) Is a Hypocrite: Evolution and the Modular Mind*. Princeton University Press.

[10]White, F. (1987). *The Overview Effect: Space Exploration and Human Evolution*. Houghton Mifflin.

[1]Frankl, V. E. (2006). *Man's Search for Meaning*. Beacon Press.

[12]Spalding, K. L., Bhardwaj, R. D., Buchholz, B. A., Druid, H., & Frisén, J. (2005). Retrospective birth dating of cells in humans. *Cell*, 122(1), 133–143.

[13]Plutarch. (1914). *Theseus*. In *The Parallel Lives* (Vol. 1). Loeb Classical Library.

[14]Kahneman, D. (2011). *Thinking, Fast and Slow*. Farrar, Straus and Giroux.

[15]Kruger, J., & Dunning, D. (1999). Unskilled and unaware of it: How difficulties in recognizing one's own incompetence lead to inflated self-assessments. *Journal of Personality and Social Psychology*, 77(6), 1121–1134.

[16]Hayes, S. C., Luoma, J. B., Bond, F. W., Masuda, A., & Lillis, J. (2006). Acceptance and commitment therapy: Model, processes and outcomes. *Behaviour Research and Therapy*, 44(1), 1–25.

Chapter Two: Our Lying Eyes

[1]Davies, R. (1983). *World of Wonders*. Viking Press.

[2]Wittgenstein, L. (1953). *Philosophical Investigations*. Blackwell.

[3]Merleau-Ponty, M. (1945). *Phenomenology of Perception*. Gallimard.

[4]Necker, L. A. (1832). Observations on some remarkable optical phenomena seen in Switzerland; and on an optical phenomenon which occurs on viewing a figure of a crystal or geometrical solid. *The London, Edinburgh, and Dublin Philosophical Magazine and Journal of Science*, 1(5), 329–337.

[5]Leopold, D. A., & Logothetis, N. K. (1999). Multistable phenomena: Changing views in perception. *Trends in Cognitive Sciences*, 3(7), 254–264.

[6]Curcio, C. A., Sloan, K. R., Kalina, R. E., & Hendrickson, A. E. (1990). Human photoreceptor topography. *Journal of Comparative Neurology*, 292(4), 497–523.

[7]Goodale, M. A., & Milner, A. D. (1992). Separate visual pathways for perception and action. *Trends in Neurosciences*, 15(1), 20–25.

NOTES

[8]Ramachandran, V. S. (1992). Blind spots. *Scientific American*, 266(5), 86–91.

[9]Cooper, W. E., & Burns, N. (1987). Social significance of ventrolateral coloration in the fence lizard, Sceloporus undulatus. *Animal Behaviour*, 35(2), 526–532.

[10]Asch, S. E. (1956). Studies of independence and conformity: I. A minority of one against a unanimous majority. *Psychological Monographs: General and Applied*, 70(9), 1–70.

[11]Berns, G. S., Chappelow, J., Zink, C. F., Pagnoni, G., Martin-Skurski, M. E., & Richards, J. (2005). Neurobiological correlates of social conformity and independence during mental rotation. *Biological Psychiatry*, 58(3), 245–253.

[12]Lorenz, K. (1943). Die angeborenen Formen möglicher Erfahrung [The innate forms of potential experience]. *Zeitschrift für Tierpsychologie*, 5(2), 235–409.

[13]Wittgenstein, L. (1921). *Tractatus Logico-Philosophicus*. Routledge & Kegan Paul.

[14]Rozin, P., Millman, L., & Nemeroff, C. (1986). Operation of the laws of sympathetic magic in disgust and other domains. *Journal of Personality and Social Psychology*, 50(4), 703–712.

[15] Korzybski, A. (1933). *Science and Sanity: An Introduction to Non-Aristotelian Systems and General Semantics*. International Non-Aristotelian Library Publishing Company.

[16] Heisenberg, W. (1958). *Physics and Philosophy: The Revolution in Modern Science*. Harper & Brothers.

[17] Ember, C. R., & Ember, M. (2011). *Cultural Anthropology* (13th ed.). Pearson.

[18] Thornhill, R., & Gangestad, S. W. (1999). Facial attractiveness. *Trends in Cognitive Sciences*, 3(12), 452–460.

[19] Langlois, J. H., Kalakanis, L., Rubenstein, A. J., Larson, A., Hallam, M., & Smoot, M. (2000). Maxims or myths of beauty? A meta-analytic and theoretical review. *Psychological Bulletin*, 126(3), 390–423.

[20] De Botton, A. (2004). *Status Anxiety*. Hamish Hamilton.

[21] Baumgartner, G. (1960). Indirect determination of the size of receptive fields in the human retina using the Hermann grid illusion. *Pflügers Archive for the Entire Physiology of Humans and Animals*, 272(1), 21–22.

[22] Anstis, S., Verstraten, F. A., & Mather, G. (1998). The motion aftereffect. *Trends in Cognitive Sciences*, 2(3), 111–117.

[23] Kanizsa, G. (1976). Subjective contours. *Scientific American*, 234(4), 48–53.

NOTES

[24]Segall, M. H., Campbell, D. T., & Herskovits, M. J. (1966). *The Influence of Culture on Visual Perception*. Bobbs-Merrill.

[25]Roberson, D., Davidoff, J., Davies, I. R., & Shapiro, L. R. (2005). Color categories: Evidence for the cultural relativity hypothesis. *Cognitive Psychology*, 50(4), 378–411.

[26]Winawer, J., Witthoft, N., Frank, M. C., Wu, L., Wade, A. R., & Boroditsky, L. (2007). Russian blues reveal effects of language on color discrimination. *Proceedings of the National Academy of Sciences*, 104(19), 7780–7785.

[27]Chokron, S., & De Agostini, M. (2000). Reading habits influence aesthetic preference. *Cognitive Brain Research*, 10(1-2), 45–49.

[28]González, C. P. (2012). Lateral organization in nineteenth-century studio photographs is influenced by the direction of writing: A comparison of Iranian and Spanish photographs. *Laterality: Asymmetries of Body, Brain and Cognition*, 17(5), 515–532.

[29]Einstein, A. (1931). Quoted in interview with G. S. Viereck, "What Life Means to Einstein," *The Saturday Evening Post*.

Chapter Three: On Our Deaf Ears

[1]Goethe, J. W. (1833). *Maxims and Reflections*. Translated by Elisabeth Stopp (1998). Penguin Classics.

[2]LeDoux, J. E. (1996). *The Emotional Brain: The Mysterious Underpinnings of Emotional Life*. Simon & Schuster.

[3]Bargh, J. A., & Chartrand, T. L. (2000). The mind in the middle: A practical guide to priming and automaticity research. In H. T. Reis & C. M. Judd (Eds.), *Handbook of Research Methods in Social and Personality Psychology* (pp. 253–285). Cambridge University Press.

[4]Bargh, J. A., Chen, M., & Burrows, L. (1996). Automaticity of social behavior: Direct effects of trait construct and stereotype activation on action. *Journal of Personality and Social Psychology*, 71(2), 230–244.

[5]Milliman, R. E. (1982). Using background music to affect the behavior of supermarket shoppers. *The Journal of Marketing*, 46(3), 86–91.

[6]Tversky, A., & Kahneman, D. (1981). The framing of decisions and the psychology of choice. *Science*, 211(4481), 453–458.

NOTES

[7] McGurk, H., & MacDonald, J. (1976). Hearing lips and seeing voices. *Nature*, 264(5588), 746–748.

[8] Deutsch, D., Henthorn, T., & Lapidis, R. (2011). Illusory transformation from speech to song. *The Journal of the Acoustical Society of America*, 129(4), 2245–2252.

[9] Cherry, E. C. (1953). Some experiments on the recognition of speech, with one and with two ears. *The Journal of the Acoustical Society of America*, 25(5), 975–979.

[10] Asch, S. E. (1952). *Social Psychology*. Prentice-Hall.

[11] Miyawaki, K., Strange, W., Verbrugge, R., Liberman, A. M., Jenkins, J. J., & Fujimura, O. (1975). An effect of linguistic experience: The discrimination of [r] and [l] by native speakers of Japanese and English. *Perception and Psychophysics*, 18(5), 331–340.

[12] Werker, J. F., & Tees, R. C. (1984). Cross-language speech perception: Evidence for perceptual reorganization during the first year of life. *Infant Behavior and Development*, 7(1), 49–63.

[13] Teachman, B. A., Smith-Janik, S. B., & Saporito, J. (2007). Information processing biases and panic disorder: Relationships among cognitive and symptom measures. *Behaviour Research and Therapy*, 45(8), 1791–1811.

[14]Spence, C. (2015). Eating with our ears: Assessing the importance of the sounds of consumption on our perception and enjoyment of multisensory flavour experiences. *Flavour*, 4(1), 3.

[15]Baguley, D., McFerran, D., & Hall, D. (2013). Tinnitus. *The Lancet*, 382(9904), 1600–1607.

[16]Waters, F., Allen, P., Aleman, A., Fernyhough, C., Woodward, T. S., Badcock, J. C., Barkus, E., Johns, L., Varese, F., Menon, M., Vercammen, A., & Larøi, F. (2012). Auditory hallucinations in schizophrenia and nonschizophrenia populations: A review and integrated model of cognitive mechanisms. *Schizophrenia Bulletin*, 38(4), 683–693.

[17]Warren, R. M. (1970). Perceptual restoration of missing speech sounds. *Science*, 167(3917), 392–393.

[18]Wittgenstein, L. (1921). *Tractatus Logico-Philosophicus*. Routledge & Kegan Paul.

[19]Whorf, B. L. (1956). *Language, Thought, and Reality: Selected Writings of Benjamin Lee Whorf*. MIT Press.

[20]Boroditsky, L. (2001). Does language shape thought? Mandarin and English speakers' conceptions of time. *Cognitive Psychology*, 43(1), 1–22.

[21] Winawer, J., Witthoft, N., Frank, M. C., Wu, L., Wade, A. R., & Boroditsky, L. (2007). Russian blues reveal effects of language on color discrimination. *Proceedings of the National Academy of Sciences*, 104(19), 7780–7785.

[22] Vygotsky, L. S. (1962). *Thought and Language*. MIT Press.

[23] Lupyan, G. (2009). Extracommunicative functions of language: Verbal interference causes selective categorization impairments. *Psychonomic Bulletin and Review*, 16(4), 711–718.

[24] Hurlburt, R. T., Heavey, C. L., & Kelsey, J. M. (2013). Toward a phenomenology of inner speaking. *Consciousness and Cognition*, 22(4), 1477–1494.

[25] Stansfeld, S. A., & Matheson, M. P. (2003). Noise pollution: Non-auditory effects on health. *British Medical Bulletin*, 68(1), 243–257.

[26] Alvarsson, J. J., Wiens, S., & Nilsson, M. E. (2010). Stress recovery during exposure to nature sound and environmental noise. *International Journal of Environmental Research and Public Health*, 7(3), 1036–1046.

[27] Lee, K. M., & Yoon, C. (2009). Sound's attention-capturing effects in distracting environments: The influence of onset and ongoing time. *Journal of the Acoustical Society of America*, 126(1), 194–198.

[28]Peretz, I., & Coltheart, M. (2003). Modularity of music processing. *Nature Neuroscience*, 6(7), 688–691.

[29]Castellano, M. A., Bharucha, J. J., & Krumhansl, C. L. (1984). Tonal hierarchies in the music of North India. *Journal of Experimental Psychology: General*, 113(3), 394–412.

[30]North, A. C., & Hargreaves, D. J. (1999). Music and adolescent identity. *Music Education Research*, 1(1), 75–92.

[31]Juslin, P. N., & Laukka, P. (2004). Expression, perception, and induction of musical emotions: A review and a questionnaire study of everyday listening. *Journal of New Music Research*, 33(3), 217–238.

[32]Thaut, M. H., McIntosh, G. C., & Hoemberg, V. (2015). Neurobiological foundations of neurologic music therapy: Rhythmic entrainment and the motor system. *Frontiers in Psychology*, 5, 1185.

[33]Meyer, L. B. (1956). *Emotion and Meaning in Music*. University of Chicago Press.

[34]Baddeley, A. D., & Hitch, G. (1974). Working memory. In G. H. Bower (Ed.), *The Psychology of Learning and Motivation* (Vol. 8, pp. 47–89). Academic Press.

NOTES

[35]Miller, G. A. (1956). The magical number seven, plus or minus two: Some limits on our capacity for processing information. *Psychological Review*, 63(2), 81–97.

[36]Samuel, A. G. (1981). Phonemic restoration: Insights from a new methodology. *Journal of Experimental Psychology: General*, 110(4), 474–494.

[37]Horowitz, S. S. (2012). *The Universal Sense: How Hearing Shapes the Mind*. Bloomsbury.

Chapter Four: Our Senses/The Senses

[1] Aquinas, T. (1947). *Summa Theologica*. Benziger Bros. (Original work from 1265-1274).

[2] Husserl, E. (1983). *Ideas Pertaining to a Pure Phenomenology and to a Phenomenological Philosophy* (F. Kersten, Trans.). Martinus Nijhoff. (Original work published 1913).

[3] Ramachandran, V. S., & Hirstein, W. (1997). Three laws of qualia: What neurology tells us about the biological functions of consciousness. *Journal of Consciousness Studies*, 4(5-6), 429–458.

[4] James, W. (1890). *The Principles of Psychology*. Henry Holt and Company.

[5] Geertz, C. (1973). *The Interpretation of Cultures*. Basic Books.

[6] Hall, E. T. (1966). *The Hidden Dimension*. Doubleday.

[7] Herz, R. S., & Schooler, J. W. (2002). A naturalistic study of autobiographical memories evoked by olfactory and visual cues: Testing the Proustian hypothesis. *The American Journal of Psychology*, 115(1), 21–32.

[8] Damasio, A. R. (1994). *Descartes' Error: Emotion, Reason, and the Human Brain*. Putnam.

NOTES

[9]Schacter, D. L., & Addis, D. R. (2007). The cognitive neuroscience of constructive memory: Remembering the past and imagining the future. *Philosophical Transactions of the Royal Society B: Biological Sciences*, 362(1481), 773–786.

[10]Rizzolatti, G., & Craighero, L. (2004). The mirror-neuron system. *Annual Review of Neuroscience*, 27, 169–192.

[11]Gallese, V., & Goldman, A. (1998). Mirror neurons and the simulation theory of mind-reading. *Trends in Cognitive Sciences*, 2(12), 493–501.

[12]Bandura, A. (1977). *Social Learning Theory*. Prentice Hall.

[13]Plassmann, H., O'Doherty, J., Shiv, B., & Rangel, A. (2008). Marketing actions can modulate neural representations of experienced pleasantness. *Proceedings of the National Academy of Sciences*, 105(3), 1050–1054.

[14]Clark, A. (2013). Whatever next? Predictive brains, situated agents, and the future of cognitive science. *Behavioral and Brain Sciences*, 36(3), 181–204.

[15]Kutas, M., & Federmeier, K. D. (2011). Thirty years and counting: Finding meaning in the N400 component of the event-related brain potential (ERP). *Annual Review of Psychology*, 62, 621–647.

[16]Helson, H. (1964). *Adaptation-Level Theory*. Harper & Row.

[17]Simons, D. J., & Chabris, C. F. (1999). Gorillas in our midst: Sustained inattentional blindness for dynamic events. *Perception*, 28(9), 1059–1074.

[18]Posner, M. I., & Petersen, S. E. (1990). The attention system of the human brain. *Annual Review of Neuroscience*, 13, 25–42.

[19]Treisman, A. M., & Gelade, G. (1980). A feature-integration theory of attention. *Cognitive Psychology*, 12(1), 97–136.

[20]Rensink, R. A., O'Regan, J. K., & Clark, J. J. (1997). To see or not to see: The need for attention to perceive changes in scenes. *Psychological Science*, 8(5), 368–373.

[21]Dalton, P., & Fraenkel, N. (2012). Gorillas we have missed: Sustained inattentional deafness for dynamic events. *Cognition*, 124(3), 367–372.

[22]Pessoa, L. (2008). On the relationship between emotion and cognition. *Nature Reviews Neuroscience*, 9(2), 148–158.

[23]Vuilleumier, P. (2005). How brains beware: Neural mechanisms of emotional attention. *Trends in Cognitive Sciences*, 9(12), 585–594.

[24]Fredrickson, B. L., & Branigan, C. (2005). Positive emotions broaden the scope of attention and thought-action repertoires. *Cognition and Emotion*, 19(3), 313–332.

[25]Beck, A. T., & Clark, D. A. (1997). An information processing model of anxiety: Automatic and strategic processes. *Behaviour Research and Therapy*, 35(1), 49–58.

[26]Haidt, J. (2001). The emotional dog and its rational tail: A social intuitionist approach to moral judgment. *Psychological Review*, 108(4), 814–834.

[27]Chapman, H. A., Kim, D. A., Susskind, J. M., & Anderson, A. K. (2009). In bad taste: Evidence for the oral origins of moral disgust. *Science*, 323(5918), 1222–1226.

[28]Graham, J., Haidt, J., & Nosek, B. A. (2009). Liberals and conservatives rely on different sets of moral foundations. *Journal of Personality and Social Psychology*, 96(5), 1029–1046.

[29]Rosch, E., & Lloyd, B. B. (Eds.). (1978). *Cognition and Categorization*. Lawrence Erlbaum Associates.

[30]Watts, A. (1957). *The Way of Zen*. Pantheon Books.

[31]Gopnik, A., Meltzoff, A. N., & Kuhl, P. K. (1999). *The Scientist in the Crib: What Early Learning Tells Us About the Mind*. Morrow.

[32]Suzuki, S. (1970). *Zen Mind, Beginner's Mind*. Weatherhill.

[33]Langer, E. J. (1989). *Mindfulness*. Da Capo Press.

[34]Aurelius, M. (2002). *Meditations* (G. Hays, Trans.). Modern Library. (Original work from 161–180 CE).

[35]Epictetus. (1995). *The Discourses* (R. Hard, Trans.). Everyman. (Original work from c. 108 CE).

[36]Beck, A. T. (1976). *Cognitive Therapy and the Emotional Disorders*. International Universities Press.

[37]Lazarus, R. S. (1991). *Emotion and Adaptation*. Oxford University Press.

[38]Gilbert, D. T., & Wilson, T. D. (2000). Miswanting: Some problems in the forecasting of future affective states. In J. P. Forgas (Ed.), *Feeling and Thinking: The Role of Affect in Social Cognition* (pp. 178-197). Cambridge University Press.

[39]Barrett, L. F. (2017). *How Emotions Are Made: The Secret Life of the Brain*. Houghton Mifflin Harcourt.

[40]Brooks, A. W. (2014). Get excited: Reappraising pre-performance anxiety as excitement. *Journal of Experimental Psychology: General*, 143(3), 1144–1158.

[41]Kant, I. (1998). *Critique of Pure Reason* (P. Guyer & A. W. Wood, Trans.). Cambridge University Press. (Original work published 1781).

[42]Seth, A. K. (2021). *Being You: A New Science of Consciousness*. Dutton.

NOTES

[43]Hoffman, D. D. (2019). *The Case Against Reality: Why Evolution Hid the Truth from Our Eyes*. Norton.

[44]Proust, M. (1923). *La Prisonnière (The Captive)*, in *À la recherche du temps perdu (In Search of Lost Time)*. Gallimard.

Chapter Five: Language

[1]Wittgenstein, L. (1921). *Tractatus Logico-Philosophicus.* Routledge & Kegan Paul.

[2]Whorf, B. L. (1956). *Language, Thought, and Reality: Selected Writings of Benjamin Lee Whorf.* MIT Press.

[3]Boroditsky, L. (2011). How language shapes thought. *Scientific American,* 304(2), 62–65.

[4]Malotki, E. (1983). *Hopi Time: A Linguistic Analysis of the Temporal Concepts in the Hopi Language.* Mouton Publishers.

[5]Gordon, P. (2004). Numerical cognition without words: Evidence from Amazonia. *Science,* 306(5695), 496–499.

[6]Winawer, J., Witthoft, N., Frank, M. C., Wu, L., Wade, A. R., & Boroditsky, L. (2007). Russian blues reveal effects of language on color discrimination. *Proceedings of the National Academy of Sciences,* 104(19), 7780–7785.

[7]Boroditsky, L., & Gaby, A. (2010). Remembrances of times East: Absolute spatial representations of time in an Australian aboriginal community. *Psychological Science,* 21(11), 1635–1639.

[8]Boroditsky, L., Schmidt, L. A., & Phillips, W. (2003). Sex, syntax, and semantics. In D. Gentner & S. Goldin-Meadow

NOTES

(Eds.), *Language in Mind: Advances in the Study of Language and Thought* (pp. 61–79). MIT Press.

[9]de Saussure, F. (1916). *Course in General Linguistics.* Philosophical Library.

[10]Boas, F. (1911). *Handbook of American Indian Languages.* Bureau of American Ethnology, Bulletin 40. Government Printing Office.

[11]Warren, R. M. (1970). Perceptual restoration of missing speech sounds. *Science,* 167(3917), 392–393.

[12]Tversky, A., & Kahneman, D. (1981). The framing of decisions and the psychology of choice. *Science,* 211(4481), 453–458.

[13]Bruner, J. (1990). *Acts of Meaning.* Harvard University Press.

[14]Pavlenko, A. (2006). Bilingual selves. In A. Pavlenko (Ed.), *Bilingual Minds: Emotional Experience, Expression, and Representation* (pp. 1–33). Multilingual Matters.

[15]Pinker, S. (2007). *The Stuff of Thought: Language as a Window into Human Nature.* Viking.

[16]Wittgenstein, L. (1953). *Philosophical Investigations.* Blackwell Publishing.

[17]Fernyhough, C. (2016). *The Voices Within: The History and Science of How We Talk to Ourselves*. Basic Books.

[18]Bermúdez, J. L. (2003). *Thinking Without Words*. Oxford University Press.

[19]Gendlin, E. T. (1978). *Focusing*. Bantam Books.

[20]de Man, P. (1978). *The Epistemology of Metaphor. Critical Inquiry*, 5(1), 13–30.

[21]Lakoff, G., & Johnson, M. (1980). *Metaphors We Live By*. University of Chicago Press.

[22]Núñez, R. E., & Sweetser, E. (2006). With the future behind them: Convergent evidence from Aymara language and gesture in the crosslinguistic comparison of spatial construals of time. *Cognitive Science*, 30(3), 401–450.

[23]Crystal, D. (2010). *The Cambridge Encyclopedia of Language* (3rd ed.). Cambridge University Press.

[24]Gee, J. P. (2014). *An Introduction to Discourse Analysis: Theory and Method* (4th ed.). Routledge.

[25]Rickford, J. R. (1999). *African American Vernacular English: Features, Evolution, Educational Implications*. Blackwell.

[26]This quote is often attributed to Orwell but without definitive source citation.

NOTES

[27]Orwell, G. (1949). *Nineteen Eighty-Four*. Secker & Warburg.

[28]Lutz, W. (1989). *Doublespeak: From "Revenue Enhancement" to "Terminal Living": How Government, Business, Advertisers, and Others Use Language to Deceive You*. Harper & Row.

[29]Cameron, D. (1998). *The Feminist Critique of Language: A Reader* (2nd ed.). Routledge.

[30]Kabat-Zinn, J. (1994). *Wherever You Go, There You Are: Mindfulness Meditation in Everyday Life*. Hyperion.

[31]Pavlenko, A. (2014). *The Bilingual Mind: And What It Tells Us about Language and Thought*. Cambridge University Press.

[32]Dickinson, E. (1960). *The Complete Poems of Emily Dickinson*. Little, Brown and Company.

[33]Baldwin, J. (1956). *Giovanni's Room*. Dial Press.

[34]Searle, J. R. (1995). *The Construction of Social Reality*. Free Press.

Chapter Six: Connection Mind/Body

[1]Nietzsche, F. (1883-1885). *Thus Spoke Zarathustra*. (Translation published 1954). Viking Press.

[2]Kandel, E. R. (2012). *The Age of Insight: The Quest to Understand the Unconscious in Art, Mind, and Brain, from Vienna 1900 to the Present*. Random House.

[3]Porges, S. W. (2011). *The Polyvagal Theory: Neurophysiological Foundations of Emotions, Attachment, Communication, and Self-regulation*. Norton.

[4]Sapolsky, R. M. (2004). *Why Zebras Don't Get Ulcers* (3rd ed.). Henry Holt and Company.

[5]Gershon, M. D. (1998). *The Second Brain: A Groundbreaking New Understanding of Nervous Disorders of the Stomach and Intestine*. HarperCollins.

[6]Armour, J. A. (2007). The little brain on the heart. *Cleveland Clinic Journal of Medicine*, 74(Suppl 1), S48–S51.

[7]McCraty, R., & Zayas, M. A. (2014). Cardiac coherence, self-regulation, autonomic stability, and psychosocial well-being. *Frontiers in Psychology*, 5, 1090.

[8]Damasio, A. R. (1994). *Descartes' Error: Emotion, Reason, and the Human Brain*. Putnam.

[9]Merleau-Ponty, M. (1945). *Phenomenology of Perception.* (Translation published 1962). Routledge & Kegan Paul.

[10]Williams, L. E., & Bargh, J. A. (2008). Experiencing physical warmth promotes interpersonal warmth. *Science,* 322(5901), 606–607.

[11]Schnall, S., Zadra, J. R., & Proffitt, D. R. (2010). Direct evidence for the economy of action: Glucose and the perception of geographical slant. *Perception,* 39(4), 464–482.

[12]Schubert, T. W., & Koole, S. L. (2009). The embodied self: Making a fist enhances men's power-related self-conceptions. *Journal of Experimental Social Psychology,* 45(4), 828–834.

[13]Wells, G. L., & Petty, R. E. (1980). The effects of overt head movements on persuasion: Compatibility and incompatibility of responses. *Basic and Applied Social Psychology,* 1(3), 219–230.

[14]Craig, A. D. (2003). Interoception: The sense of the physiological condition of the body. *Current Opinion in Neurobiology,* 13(4), 500–505.

[15]Critchley, H. D., & Garfinkel, S. N. (2017). Interoception and emotion. *Current Opinion in Psychology,* 17, 7–14.

[16]Damasio, A. R. (1996). The somatic marker hypothesis and the possible functions of the prefrontal cortex. *Philosophical Transactions of the Royal Society of London. Series B: Biological Sciences*, 351(1346), 1413–1420.

[17]Bechara, A., Damasio, H., Tranel, D., & Damasio, A. R. (1997). Deciding advantageously before knowing the advantageous strategy. *Science*, 275(5304), 1293–1295.

[18]McEwen, B. S. (2007). Physiology and neurobiology of stress and adaptation: Central role of the brain. *Physiological Reviews*, 87(3), 873–904.

[19]McEwen, B. S., & Stellar, E. (1993). Stress and the individual: Mechanisms leading to disease. *Archives of Internal Medicine*, 153(18), 2093–2101.

[20]The American Institute of Stress. (2020). *Stress Research*. https://www.stress.org/stress-research

[21]Ader, R. (2007). *Psychoneuroimmunology* (4th ed.). Academic Press.

[22]Cohen, S., Janicki-Deverts, D., Doyle, W. J., Miller, G. E., Frank, E., Rabin, B. S., & Turner, R. B. (2012). Chronic stress, glucocorticoid receptor resistance, inflammation, and disease risk. *Proceedings of the National Academy of Sciences*, 109(16), 5995–5999.

[23] Epel, E. S., Blackburn, E. H., Lin, J., Dhabhar, F. S., Adler, N. E., Morrow, J. D., & Cawthon, R. M. (2004). Accelerated telomere shortening in response to life stress. *Proceedings of the National Academy of Sciences*, 101(49), 17312–17315.

[24] Li, Q. (2010). Effect of forest bathing trips on human immune function. *Environmental Health and Preventive Medicine*, 15(1), 9–17.

[25] Ulrich, R. S. (1984). View through a window may influence recovery from surgery. *Science*, 224(4647), 420–421.

[26] Nieuwenhuis, M., Knight, C., Postmes, T., & Haslam, S. A. (2014). The relative benefits of green versus lean office space: Three field experiments. *Journal of Experimental Psychology: Applied*, 20(3), 199–214.

[27] Hunter, M. R., Gillespie, B. W., & Chen, S. Y. (2019). Urban nature experiences reduce stress in the context of daily life based on salivary biomarkers. *Frontiers in Psychology*, 10, 722.

[28] Wilson, E. O. (1984). *Biophilia*. Harvard University Press.

[29] Kaplan, S. (1995). The restorative benefits of nature: Toward an integrative framework. *Journal of Environmental Psychology*, 15(3), 169–182.

[30]Pearson, D. G., & Craig, T. (2014). The great outdoors? Exploring the mental health benefits of natural environments. *Frontiers in Psychology*, 5, 1178.

[31]Miller, A. (1981). *The Drama of the Gifted Child: The Search for the True Self*. Basic Books.

[32]van der Kolk, B. A. (2014). *The Body Keeps the Score: Brain, Mind, and Body in the Healing of Trauma*. Viking.

[33]Maté, G. (2003). *When the Body Says No: Understanding the Stress-Disease Connection*. Wiley.

[34]Rankin, L. (2013). *Mind Over Medicine: Scientific Proof That You Can Heal Yourself*. Hay House.

[35]Keleman, S. (1985). *Emotional Anatomy*. Center Press.

[36]Lowen, A. (1958). *The Language of the Body*. Grune & Stratton.

[37]Levine, P. A. (1997). *Waking the Tiger: Healing Trauma*. North Atlantic Books.

[38]Lanius, R. A., Vermetten, E., & Pain, C. (Eds.). (2010). *The Impact of Early Life Trauma on Health and Disease: The Hidden Epidemic*. Cambridge University Press.

[39]Ader, R., & Cohen, N. (1975). Behaviorally conditioned immunosuppression. *Psychosomatic Medicine*, 37(4), 333–340.

[40]Sternberg, E. M. (2000). *The Balance Within: The Science Connecting Health and Emotions.* W. H. Freeman.

[41]Mayer, E. A. (2011). Gut feelings: The emerging biology of gut–brain communication. *Nature Reviews Neuroscience,* 12(8), 453–466.

[42]Fredrickson, B. L., & Losada, M. F. (2005). Positive affect and the complex dynamics of human flourishing. *American Psychologist,* 60(7), 678–686.

[43]Davidson, R. J., & Kasgniak, A. W. (2015). Conceptual and methodological issues in research on mindfulness and meditation. *American Psychologist,* 70(7), 581–592.

[44]Kabat-Zinn, J. (1990). *Full Catastrophe Living: Using the Wisdom of Your Body and Mind to Face Stress, Pain, and Illness.* Delacorte Press.

[45]Grossman, P., Niemann, L., Schmidt, S., & Walach, H. (2004). Mindfulness-based stress reduction and health benefits: A meta-analysis. *Journal of Psychosomatic Research,* 57(1), 35–43.

[46]Farb, N., Daubenmier, J., Price, C. J., Gard, T., Kerr, C., Dunn, B. D., Klein, A. C., Paulus, M. P., & Mehling, W. E. (2015). Interoception, contemplative practice, and health. *Frontiers in Psychology,* 6, 763.

[47]Salmon, P., Lush, E., Jablonski, M., & Sephton, S. E. (2009). Yoga and mindfulness: Clinical aspects of an ancient mind/body practice. *Cognitive and Behavioral Practice*, 16(1), 59–72.

[48]Jahnke, R., Larkey, L., Rogers, C., Etnier, J., & Lin, F. (2010). A comprehensive review of health benefits of qigong and tai chi. *American Journal of Health Promotion*, 24(6), e1–e25.

[49]Buchanan, P. A., & Ulrich, B. D. (2001). The Feldenkrais Method: A dynamic approach to changing motor behavior. *Research Quarterly for Exercise and Sport*, 72(4), 315–323.

[50]Halprin, A. (2000). *Dance as a Healing Art: Returning to Health with Movement and Imagery*. LifeRhythm.

[51]Brown, R. P., & Gerbarg, P. L. (2012). *The Healing Power of the Breath: Simple Techniques to Reduce Stress and Anxiety, Enhance Concentration, and Balance Your Emotions*. Shambhala Publications.

[52]Zaccaro, A., Piarulli, A., Laurino, M., Garbella, E., Menicucci, D., Neri, B., & Gemignani, A. (2018). How breath-control can change your life: A systematic review on psycho-physiological correlates of slow breathing. *Frontiers in Human Neuroscience*, 12, 353.

[53]Telles, S., Sharma, S. K., & Balkrishna, A. (2014). Blood pressure and heart rate variability during yoga-based

alternate nostril breathing practice and breath awareness. *Medical Science Monitor Basic Research*, 20, 184–193.

[54]van der Kolk, B. A. (2006). Clinical implications of neuroscience research in PTSD. *Annals of the New York Academy of Sciences*, 1071(1), 277–293.

[55]Levine, P. A. (2010). *In an Unspoken Voice: How the Body Releases Trauma and Restores Goodness*. North Atlantic Books.

[56]Ogden, P., Minton, K., & Pain, C. (2006). *Trauma and the Body: A Sensorimotor Approach to Psychotherapy*. Norton.

[57]Shapiro, F. (2018). *Eye Movement Desensitization and Reprocessing (EMDR) Therapy: Basic Principles, Protocols, and Procedures* (3rd ed.). Guilford.

[58]Emerson, D., & Hopper, E. (2011). *Overcoming Trauma through Yoga: Reclaiming Your Body*. North Atlantic Books.

[59]Graham, M. (1991). *Blood Memory: An Autobiography*. Doubleday.

Chapter Seven: Relationships

[1] Nin, A. (1961). *Seduction of the Minotaur*. Swallow Press.

[2] Lieberman, M. D. (2013). *Social: Why Our Brains Are Wired to Connect*. Crown.

[3] Johnson, M. H., Dziurawiec, S., Ellis, H., & Morton, J. (1991). Newborns' preferential tracking of face-like stimuli and its subsequent decline. *Cognition*, 40(1-2), 1–19.

[4] Rizzolatti, G., & Craighero, L. (2004). The mirror-neuron system. *Annual Review of Neuroscience*, 27, 169–192.

[5] Kanwisher, N., McDermott, J., & Chun, M. M. (1997). The fusiform face area: A module in human extrastriate cortex specialized for face perception. *Journal of Neuroscience*, 17(11), 4302–4311.

[6] Feldman, R. (2012). Parent-infant synchrony: A biobehavioral model of mutual influences in the formation of affiliative bonds. *Monographs of the Society for Research in Child Development*, 77(2), 42–51.

[7] Holt-Lunstad, J., Smith, T. B., & Layton, J. B. (2010). Social relationships and mortality risk: A meta-analytic review. *PLoS Medicine*, 7(7), e1000316.

NOTES

[8]Holt-Lunstad, J., Smith, T. B., Baker, M., Harris, T., & Stephenson, D. (2015). Loneliness and social isolation as risk factors for mortality: A meta-analytic review. *Perspectives on Psychological Science,* 10(2), 227–237.

[9]Jung, C. G. (1964). *Man and His Symbols.* Doubleday.

[10]Bowlby, J. (1969). *Attachment and Loss: Vol. 1. Attachment.* Basic Books.

[11]Doidge, N. (2007). *The Brain That Changes Itself: Stories of Personal Triumph from the Frontiers of Brain Science.* Viking.

[12]Freud, S. (1920). Beyond the pleasure principle. In J. Strachey (Ed. & Trans.), *The Standard Edition of the Complete Psychological Works of Sigmund Freud* (Vol. 18, pp. 1-64). Hogarth Press.

[13]Firestone, R. W., & Catlett, J. (1999). *Fear of Intimacy.* American Psychological Association.

[14]Frith, C. D., & Frith, U. (2006). The neural basis of mentalizing. *Neuron,* 50(4), 531–534.

[15]Gallese, V., & Goldman, A. (1998). Mirror neurons and the simulation theory of mind-reading. *Trends in Cognitive Sciences,* 2(12), 493–501.

[16]Lutz, A., Brefczynski-Lewis, J., Johnstone, T., & Davidson, R. J. (2008). Regulation of the neural circuitry of emotion by

compassion meditation: Effects of meditative expertise. *PLoS ONE*, 3(3), e1897.

[17]Shapiro, S. L., Carlson, L. E., Astin, J. A., & Freedman, B. (2006). Mechanisms of mindfulness. *Journal of Clinical Psychology*, 62(3), 373–386.

[18]Davis, M. H. (1983). Measuring individual differences in empathy: Evidence for a multidimensional approach. *Journal of Personality and Social Psychology*, 44(1), 113–126.

[19]Galinsky, A. D., & Moskowitz, G. B. (2000). Perspective-taking: Decreasing stereotype expression, stereotype accessibility, and in-group favoritism. *Journal of Personality and Social Psychology*, 78(4), 708–724.

[20]Von Neumann, J., & Morgenstern, O. (1944). *Theory of Games and Economic Behavior*. Princeton University Press.

[21]Rogers, C. R. (1961). *On Becoming a Person: A Therapist's View of Psychotherapy*. Houghton Mifflin.

[22]Bowen, M. (1978). *Family Therapy in Clinical Practice*. Jason Aronson.

[23]Krishnamurti, J. (1996). *Total Freedom: The Essential Krishnamurti*. HarperOne.

[24]Jung, C. G. (1951). Fundamental questions of psychotherapy. In H. Read, M. Fordham, & G. Adler (Eds.),

NOTES

The Collected Works of C. G. Jung (Vol. 16, pp. 111-125). Princeton University Press.

[25]Holden, R. (2007). *Success Intelligence: Essential Lessons and Practices from the World's Leading Coaching Program on Authentic Success.* Hay House.

[26]Singer, T., & Klimecki, O. M. (2014). Empathy and compassion. *Current Biology,* 24(18), R875–R878.

[27]Klimecki, O. M., Leiberg, S., Lamm, C., & Singer, T. (2013). Functional neural plasticity and associated changes in positive affect after compassion training. *Cerebral Cortex,* 23(7), 1552–1561.

[28]Neff, K. D. (2003). Self-compassion: An alternative conceptualization of a healthy attitude toward oneself. *Self and Identity,* 2(2), 85–101.

[29]Neff, K. D., & Vonk, R. (2009). Self-compassion versus global self-esteem: Two different ways of relating to oneself. *Journal of Personality,* 77(1), 23–50.

[30]Rogers, C. R. (1957). The necessary and sufficient conditions of therapeutic personality change. *Journal of Consulting Psychology,* 21(2), 95–103.

[31]Bartholomew, K., & Horowitz, L. M. (1991). Attachment styles among young adults: A test of a four-category model. *Journal of Personality and Social Psychology*, 61(2), 226–244.

[32]Lerner, H. G. (1989). *The Dance of Intimacy: A Woman's Guide to Courageous Acts of Change in Key Relationships*. Harper & Row.

[33]Schnarch, D. (1997). *Passionate Marriage: Keeping Love and Intimacy Alive in Committed Relationships*. Henry Holt and Company.

[34]Mehrabian, A. (1972). *Nonverbal Communication*. Aldine-Atherton.

[35]Stern, D. N. (1985). *The Interpersonal World of the Infant: A View from Psychoanalysis and Developmental Psychology*. Basic Books.

[36]Rogers, C. R. (1961). *On Becoming a Person: A Therapist's View of Psychotherapy*. Houghton Mifflin.

[37]Whyte, D. (2002). *The Heart Aroused: Poetry and the Preservation of the Soul in Corporate America*. Currency Doubleday.

[38]Verduyn, P., Ybarra, O., Résibois, M., Jonides, J., & Kross, E. (2017). Do social network sites enhance or undermine

subjective well-being? A critical review. *Social Issues and Policy Review*, 11(1), 274–302.

[39]Przybylski, A. K., & Weinstein, N. (2013). Can you connect with me now? How the presence of mobile communication technology influences face-to-face conversation quality. *Journal of Social and Personal Relationships*, 30(3), 237–246.

[40]Kushlev, K., & Dunn, E. W. (2019). Smartphones distract parents from cultivating feelings of connection when spending time with their children. *Journal of Social and Personal Relationships*, 36(6), 1619–1639.

[41]Pariser, E. (2011). *The Filter Bubble: What the Internet Is Hiding from You*. Penguin Press.

[42]Alter, A. (2017). *Irresistible: The Rise of Addictive Technology and the Business of Keeping Us Hooked*. Penguin Press.

[43]Kruger, J., Epley, N., Parker, J., & Ng, Z. W. (2005). Egocentrism over e-mail: Can we communicate as well as we think? *Journal of Personality and Social Psychology*, 89(6), 925–936.

[44]Vogel, E. A., Rose, J. P., Roberts, L. R., & Eckles, K. (2014). Social comparison, social media, and self-esteem. *Psychology of Popular Media Culture*, 3(4), 206–222.

[45] Bailenson, J. N. (2021). Nonverbal overload: A theoretical argument for the causes of Zoom fatigue. *Technology, Mind, and Behavior*, 2(1).

[46] Jung, C. G. (1933). *Modern Man in Search of a Soul*. Harcourt Brace.

NOTES

Chapter Eight: The Absolute Truth

[1]Nietzsche, F. (1901). *The Will to Power*. (Translation published 1967). Vintage Books.

[2]Sagan, C. (1980). *Cosmos*. Random House.

[3]Sagan, C. (1977). *The Dragons of Eden: Speculations on the Evolution of Human Intelligence*. Random House.

[4]Swimme, B., & Berry, T. (1992). *The Universe Story: From the Primordial Flaring Forth to the Ecozoic Era—A Celebration of the Unfolding of the Cosmos*. HarperOne.

[5]Chalmers, D. J. (1995). Facing up to the problem of consciousness. *Journal of Consciousness Studies*, 2(3), 200–219.

[6]Feynman, R. P. (1965). *The Feynman Lectures on Physics, Vol. III: Quantum Mechanics*. Addison-Wesley.

[7]Hoffman, D. D. (2019). *The Case Against Reality: Why Evolution Hid the Truth from Our Eyes*. Norton.

[8]Wittmann, M. (2016). *Felt Time: The Psychology of How We Perceive Time*. MIT Press.

[9]Einstein, A. (Attributed). While there's no verified source for this exact quote, Einstein frequently used similar examples to explain relativity in non-technical terms.

[10]Yalom, I. D. (2008). *Staring at the Sun: Overcoming the Terror of Death*. Jossey-Bass.

[11]Seneca. (2007). *Dialogues and Essays* (J. Davie, Trans.). Oxford University Press. (Original work from c. 50 CE).

[12]Smith, J. E. (1969). Time, Times, and the "Right Time": *Chronos* and *Kairos*. *The Monist*, 53(1), 1–13.

[13]Nhat Hanh, T. (1991). *Peace is Every Step: The Path of Mindfulness in Everyday Life*. Bantam.

[14]Goleman, D. (1995). *Emotional Intelligence: Why It Can Matter More Than IQ*. Bantam.

[15]Kabat-Zinn, J. (1994). *Wherever You Go, There You Are: Mindfulness Meditation in Everyday Life*. Hyperion.

[16]Masters, R. A. (2006). *Spiritual Bypassing: When Spirituality Disconnects Us from What Really Matters*. North Atlantic Books.

[17]Mesquita, B., Barrett, L. F., & Smith, E. R. (Eds.). (2010). *The Mind in Context*. Guilford.

[18]Barrett, L. F. (2017). *How Emotions Are Made: The Secret Life of the Brain*. Houghton Mifflin Harcourt.

[19]Greenberg, L. S. (2015). *Emotion-Focused Therapy: Coaching Clients to Work Through Their Feelings* (2nd ed.). American Psychological Association.

[20]David, S. (2016). *Emotional Agility: Get Unstuck, Embrace Change, and Thrive in Work and Life.* Avery.

[21]Dunbar, R. I. M. (1992). Neocortex size as a constraint on group size in primates. *Journal of Human Evolution, 22*(6), 469–493.

[22]Richerson, P. J., & Boyd, R. (2005). *Not By Genes Alone: How Culture Transformed Human Evolution.* University of Chicago Press.

[23]Harari, Y. N. (2014). *Sapiens: A Brief History of Humankind.* Harper.

[24]Shweder, R. A., Much, N. C., Mahapatra, M., & Park, L. (1997). The "big three" of morality (autonomy, community, divinity) and the "big three" explanations of suffering. In A. M. Brandt & P. Rozin (Eds.), *Morality and Health* (pp. 119-169). Routledge.

[25]Haidt, J. (2012). *The Righteous Mind: Why Good People Are Divided by Politics and Religion.* Pantheon.

[26]Greene, J. (2013). *Moral Tribes: Emotion, Reason, and the Gap Between Us and Them.* Penguin Press.

[27] Wolf, S. (1982). Moral saints. *The Journal of Philosophy*, 79(8), 419–439.

[28] Singer, P. (1981). *The Expanding Circle: Ethics, Evolution, and Moral Progress*. Princeton University Press.

[29] Appiah, K. A. (2006). *Cosmopolitanism: Ethics in a World of Strangers*. Norton.

[30] Plato. (1974). *The Republic* (D. Lee, Trans.). Penguin Books. (Original work from c. 380 BCE).

[31] Freud, A. (1936). *The Ego and the Mechanisms of Defense*. International Universities Press.

[32] Becker, E. (1973). *The Denial of Death*. Free Press.

[33] Festinger, L. (1957). *A Theory of Cognitive Dissonance*. Stanford University Press.

[34] Laing, R. D. (1967). *The Politics of Experience*. Pantheon.

[35] Wilber, K. (2000). *A Brief History of Everything* (2nd ed.). Shambhala Publications.

[36] Sartre, J.P. (1946). *Existentialism Is a Humanism* (C. Macomber, Trans., 2007). Yale University Press.

[37] Frankl, V. E. (2006). *Man's Search for Meaning*. Beacon Press. (Original work published 1946).

NOTES

[38]Buber, M. (1970). *I and Thou* (W. Kaufmann, Trans.). Charles Scribner's Sons. (Original work published 1923).

[39]Bohr, N. (1949). Discussion with Einstein on epistemological problems in atomic physics. In P. A. Schilpp (Ed.), *Albert Einstein: Philosopher-Scientist* (pp. 199-241). Library of Living Philosophers.

[40]Dennett, D. C. (2003). *Freedom Evolves*. Viking.

[41]Sagan, C. (1994). *Pale Blue Dot: A Vision of the Human Future in Space*. Random House.

[42]Swimme, B. (1995). *The Hidden Heart of the Cosmos: Humanity and the New Story*. Orbis Books.

[43]Camus, A. (1955). *The Myth of Sisyphus and Other Essays* (J. O'Brien, Trans.). Knopf. (Original work published 1942).

[44]Sartre, J. P. (1943). *Being and Nothingness* (H. E. Barnes, Trans., 1956). Philosophical Library.

[45]Sartre, J.P. (1946). *Existentialism Is a Humanism* (C. Macomber, Trans., 2007). Yale University Press.

[46]Baumeister, R. F., & Landau, M. J. (2018). Finding the meaning of meaning: Emerging insights on four grand questions. *Review of General Psychology*, 22(1), 1–10.

[47]Dawkins, R. (1998). *Unweaving the Rainbow: Science, Delusion and the Appetite for Wonder*. Houghton Mifflin.

www.ingramcontent.com/pod-product-compliance
Lightning Source LLC
Chambersburg PA
CBHW041216130526
44582CB00025BA/35